New York and the China Trade

Cover: *View of New York*, 1802, drawn and published by William Birch of Pennsylvania and etched by Samuel Seymour. An anonymous artist in Canton painted a copy of this print onto the inside of the large punch bowl that General Jacob Morton presented to the Corporation of the City of New York on July 4, 1812 (cat. c71). Collection of The New-York Historical Society.

New York and the China Trade

David Sanctuary Howard

With an essay by
Conrad Edick Wright

The New-York Historical Society
1984

Published in association with Columbia Publishing Co., Inc., Frenchtown, New Jersey

The New-York Historical Society gratefully acknowledges grants from The Vincent Astor Foundation, The Hongkong and Shanghai Banking Corporation, Atlantic Richfield Foundation, and The Armand G. Erpf Fund which helped to make this exhibition possible.

Contents

Lenders to the Exhibition

Abigail Adams Smith Museum
Albany Institute of History and Art
The American Numismatic Society
Art Commission of the City of New York
Mr. and Mrs. Charles A. Atkins
William Nathaniel Banks
Dr. Robert S. Beekman
Berry-Hill Galleries
Keith L. Black
Brooklyn Museum
Mrs. Joseph A. Burton
China Trade Museum
Mr. and Mrs. Joseph C. Cockrell, Jr.
Cooper-Hewitt Museum
Mrs. Marjorie Van Schaick Emerson
Dr. John Quentin Feller
Fine Arts Committee,
    United States Department of State
The Fleck House
    (The Dietrich Brothers Americana
    Corporation)
Henry Ford Museum and Greenfield
    Village, The Edison Institute
Florence Clark Frank
Reuben Getschow
Peter Trowbridge Gill
Dr. Alan Granby
Governor and Mrs. W. Averell Harriman
Historic Cherry Hill
George M. Kaufman
Charles Burr Lamar
Bernard and S. Dean Levy
Francis H. Low
Mr. and Mrs. Alvin Mann
Maryland Hall of Records

Metropolitan Museum of Art
Robert B. Minturn
Morristown National Historical Park
Mrs. Mildred Mottahedeh
National Society of Colonial Dames
The New Jersey State Museum
New York City Landmarks Preservation
    Commission
New York Public Library
New York State Office of Parks,
    Recreation and Historic Preservation,
    Bureau of Historic Sites
    —Clermont State Historic Site
    —John Jay Homestead Historic Site
    —Division for Historic Preservation
Newark Museum
Peabody Museum of Salem
Preservation Society of Newport County
Redwood Library and Athenaeum
Mr. and Mrs. Samuel Schwartz
Sleepy Hollow Restorations,
    Tarrytown, New York
R. M. Smythe and Co., Inc.
Swig, Weiler, and Arnow
United States Department of the Interior,
    National Park Service,
    Home of Franklin D. Roosevelt
    National Historic Site, Vanderbilt
    Mansion National Historic Site
Mrs. Thomas E. Ward
Washington and Lee University,
    The Reeves Collection
Mrs. Phoebe D. Williams
Erving and Joyce Wolf
Eight anonymous lenders

Board of Trustees

Preface

The opening of a major exhibition is always a significant occasion for the institution that has organized it. The opening of "New York and the China Trade," the culmination of months of effort, is attended not only with the excitement that always accompanies such an event, but with an additional interest as it announces a new direction in the Society's exhibitions.

Members of the Society are aware of the broad diversity of its holdings, which include important collections of portraits, landscape and genre paintings, silver objects, sculpture, furniture, books, manuscripts, prints, and photographs. The variety of the Society's collections affords an opportunity to approach the theme of a major exhibition from more than one direction. In organizing "New York and the China Trade" the intention has been to present many beautiful and striking Chinese imports—including porcelain, lacquer ware, carved ivory, and other objects—in their proper historical context. Objects from our own rich collections, with the addition of loans both from individuals and institutions, have been fashioned by David S. Howard, guest curator, and the staff of the Society into an exhibition which will fascinate those who want to learn more about the history of New York and the decorative arts.

Robert G. Goelet
President

Introduction

"New York and the China Trade" commemorates the bicentennial of an adventure. When the *Empress of China* set sail for Canton on February 22, 1784, she began an exciting era in the history of our city and state. Never before had an American vessel ventured to China. Rumor and hearsay had been New York's primary sources of information about the Orient before the voyage of this 360-ton merchant ship. When she dropped anchor in New York harbor on May 11, 1785, nearly fifteen months after she had passed the lighthouse at Sandy Hook and set her course for China, the *Empress of China* announced important news: the establishment of relations both commercial and cultural between the world's youngest nation, its independence secured only a few years before, and perhaps the oldest.

The voyage had revealed a society utterly unlike New York's. At the same time, it had opened new opportunities for speculation and profit. In the years that followed, the "China trade," the commerce with Canton that the *Empress of China* initiated, became a staple of the American economy and the basis of many of the greatest mercantile fortunes amassed during the nineteenth century.

Today, the term "China trade" often brings to mind treasured porcelain services behind glass doors in dining rooms and pantries, carefully preserved and handed down for generations, as well as fine pieces on exhibition in museums of history and art. Our reflexive identification of the China trade with porcelain is a modern development, however, one that would have surprised New Yorkers a century ago. In their minds, the China trade also meant tea, as well as spices, lacquer ware, fine silks, rough cottons, wicker mats, firecrackers, sugar candy, and countless other imports.

In organizing "New York and the China Trade," David S. Howard, the exhibition's guest curator, and the staff of The New-York Historical Society have paid attention both to the trade's history and to its contributions to the decorative arts. With only a few exceptions, the pieces on exhibition have proven New York histories. Porcelain necessarily plays a major role, but not to the exclusion of carved ivory and soapstone, lacquer ware, silver, nautical ephemera, documents, and many other reminders of the history of New York's China trade. The objective is a study of a major aspect of New York's taste over several centuries placed in its historical setting, the story of the port's trade with China.

"New York and the China Trade" could not have been organized without the help of many friends of The New-York Historical Society. It is the pleasantest of obligations to acknowledge the contributions of the following: Warren D. Beach; Terry Blake; Mrs. Henry S. Brown; Joseph T. Butler; Lucy J. B. Butler; Jacqueline Calder; John A. Cherol; Clement E. Conger; Theodore Corbett; Suzanne C. Crilley; Susan R. Cummings; Phillip Curtis; Susan Davis; Ulysses Dietz; Thomas M. Doerflinger; Frances von Stade Downing; Leslie Elam; H. A. Crosby Forbes; Alice Cooney Frelinghuysen; Pie Friendly; Glenda S. Galt; Donald T. Gibbs; Lisa Gwirtzman; Mrs. Norbert Hansen; Patricia E. Harris; Donna Hassler; Diane

E. Herzog; Fred Hill; Rose C. Houston; Paul R. Huey; Meta Janowitz; Kate Johnson; William Keller; Paul Kengla; Joyce P. Kobasa; Audrey Koenig; Susan Kupczynski; Clare Le Corbeiller; John J. McCusker; Kathryn A. McCutchen; David Revere McFadden; Donald H. McTernan; Samuel C. Miller; Bruce Naramore; Christina H. Nelson; Edward C. Papenfuse; Heather Reay; Deborah McCracken Rebuck; David L. Reese; Norman S. Rice; Nancy E. Richards; Alexandra W. Rollins; Christine Robinson; John Robinson; Nan Rothschild; Frances Gruber Safford; Karol A. Schmiegel; Paul G. Schneider, Jr.; Leah P. Sloshberg; Romaine S. Somerville; Robert Springer; Roxanne Hatfield Squibbs; Kevin Stayton; John D. Stinson; Suzanne C. Stirn; Jeffrey W. Strean; Mary S. Ushay; James W. Whitehead; Jacquelyn Wong; and Walter Zervas.

James B. Bell
Director

New York and the China Trade

Merchants and Mandarins:
New York and the Early China Trade

Conrad Edick Wright

A View of the City of New-York from Brooklyn Heights. "Pantograph" by Julien St. Mermin, 1798. Collection of The New-York Historical Society.

The Empress of China

On a wooden wharf jutting into New York's East River, a gang of burly stevedores wrestled bulky chests and boxes onto the wagons that would cart them to a nearby warehouse. Aboard the 360-ton sailing ship alongside the pier, a second crew hoisted more crates and bales from her holds. Nearly fifteen months after she had ventured from New York for the Pearl River and Canton, the *Empress of China* was home.

Laden with furs, lead, wine, tar, turpentine, casks of silver dollars, and ginseng, a medicinal root prized in the Orient, the *Empress of China* had set sail from New York on February 22, 1784. As Captain John Green had promenaded the vessel past the Battery at the southern tip of Manhattan, she had fired off a thirteen-gun salute and received a twelve-gun reply. More than 32,000 nautical miles later, on May 11, 1785, carrying a cargo of tea, nankeens, silk, porcelain, and cassia, a coarse cinnamon bark, she had repeated her salute on reentering New York harbor.[1]

It had been a successful voyage. The outbound cargo that Robert Morris of Philadelphia and Daniel Parker, William Duer, and John Holker of New York had assembled had cost them $120,000. Samuel Shaw of Boston and Thomas Randall of New York, the investors' agents or "supercargoes" aboard the *Empress of China*, had sold these wares at such good prices in Canton that Randall had leased a second vessel, the *Pallas*, to carry additional freight home. When they finally closed their books on the venture, Morris and his partners could boast a profit of $30,727, or a return of better than twenty-five percent.[2]

A successful voyage was always good reason for celebration and congratulation, especially one that paid off so handsomely. This one was unusual, however, a cause for added excitement.

When the *Empress of China* had sailed past the centuries-old Portuguese colony at

Macao, up the Pearl River, through its maze of islands called the Bocca Tigris or Tiger's Mouth, and dropped anchor at Whampoa, twelve miles downstream of Canton, the only city to which the Chinese admitted western traders, she had become the first American vessel to navigate as far as this vast and ancient empire. Her return home deserved the stir it caused. This was an occasion for celebration, an event so exciting that one New York newspaper called for "public thanksgiving and ringing of bells!"[3]

The *Empress of China* had opened direct relations between the United States, the world's youngest nation, and China, perhaps the oldest. Only five months before she sailed, the signing of the Treaty of Paris had concluded the Revolutionary War and assured American independence. In this context, the voyage was doubly symbolic, expressing American aspirations for acceptance by the world's great powers as an equal partner both in international trade and in diplomacy. The voyage had introduced American merchants to an important new market, one that would comprise one-seventh of the nation's foreign trade by 1790,[4] while at the same time it had established contacts between two distant and different peoples.

Ambitious merchants like Morris, Parker, Duer, and Holker recognized another of the voyage's lessons: there were substantial fortunes to be made in the China trade. Of course, there were also risks, daunting ones, as any prudent investor had to admit. As a business proposition, the China trade offered opportunities for speculative investments in 1785, not secure returns. If great profits beckoned, the specter of equally significant losses haunted a plunger's more insecure moments.

This was a time of national optimism, however, a time to find the best in every new development. Independence from one of the world's great colonial powers, the successful establishment of democratic governments in each of the thirteen states, and encouraging reports from Ohio and Kentucky which described fertile farmland awaiting settlers had all accustomed Americans to good news. Now, thanks to the *Empress of China*, an ancient and exotic nation lay open to American commerce. What better evidence could there be that "a future happy period"[5] was in store for the new nation?

Colonial New York and the China Trade

It was peculiarly fitting that the first vessel to venture between the United States and China had sailed out of New York harbor. Although the voyage of the *Empress of China* had opened direct relations between the two nations, New York had maintained indirect connections with China for a century and three-quarters. As the China trade matured, moreover, New York was destined by the 1830s to become its principal American port. To be sure, New York's ties to China had been quite fragile at first, more accidental than intentional. Ironically, the city's settlement itself had been in part the result of a misdirected Dutch attempt to find the fabled Northwest Passage, a rumored water route through the North American continent to the Pacific and China. And only toward the middle of the eighteenth century had the volume of New York's commerce in China goods, arriving by way of British ports, grown to more than negligible levels. Nevertheless, more than any other American city or town, New York's colonial past had been connected with China and the city's future would be influenced by their strengthening relationship.

Samuel Shaw (1754–1794), supercargo of the *Empress of
China*. Oil on canvas by H. R. Burdick after the
original attributed to John Johnston, early twentieth
century. Collection of Mr. and Mrs. Robert B.
Minturn.

New York's merchants welcomed opportunities in 1784 unlike any that had ever been open
to them. Representatives from Great Britain and the United States had required only a few
minutes the previous year to sign the Treaty of Paris, but their signatures had transformed
American commerce. Between its settlement in 1624 and the Declaration of Independence in
1776, New York had belonged successively to two European powers, first the Netherlands until
1664, and then England until the American Revolution. Each of these nations had made demands on its colonies and had burdened them with restrictive mercantile regulations. In each
case, a small coterie of wealthy European merchants had controlled colonial New York's contacts with the Far East and limited the city's prospects for oriental trade. Before 1775 the best
vantage points for observing New York's commerce with China had consequently been the
centers of the two mercantile systems to which the city had belonged, Amsterdam and London.

The Dutch had come to the China trade relatively late. Storied names like Kublai Khan,
the thirteenth-century Mongol emperor of China, and Marco Polo, the Italian merchant and
explorer whose travels in China covered the period 1271 to 1295, dominate the history of the
trade's earliest years. Dutch interest in direct commerce with China, however, did not develop
until the mid-1590s. Before 1594, the Netherlands had satisfied its desire for Chinese spices,
silks, and porcelain through trade with the Portuguese, who had monopolized maritime routes
to the Orient since the early sixteenth century and had established Macao, a permanent colony
near the mouth of the Pearl River, in 1557. In 1594, however, the Portuguese had closed the
port of Lisbon to the Netherlands, compelling Dutch merchants to risk direct commerce with
China if they desired any commerce at all.[6]

At first, Dutch ships bound for the Orient followed the Portuguese routes, south to the
Cape of Good Hope, then east past Madagascar, across the Indian Ocean, through the Indo-

nesian islands, and north to the south China coast. This was a long and treacherous journey, however, across stormy waters, and Dutch merchants soon began to consider the possibility of a faster, safer, and more profitable passage westward across the Atlantic and Pacific to China. The Dutch East India Company took the initiative in 1609.

The Company had been established in 1602, receiving from its government a monopoly of trade between Dutch ports and the east. This franchise already held a lucrative potential, but if there were a way to shorten voyages and reduce costs, then its value promised to soar.

The Dutch were not the first Europeans to search for a westward route to China. That had been Christopher Columbus's objective in 1492. Over the course of the intervening century many explorers in quest of the Northwest Passage had probed the largest bays and rivers along North America's Atlantic coast. In fact, Henry Hudson, the English navigator whom the Dutch East India Company retained in 1609, was already a veteran of two such voyages, in 1585 and 1607.

Hudson's first two voyages had followed northerly courses in search of an Arctic route to the Orient. Rumors circulating along Amsterdam's docks in 1609, however, had hinted of two other possible passages. One was north of modern-day Labrador and through what is now called Hudson Strait, which connects the Atlantic and Hudson Bay. The second was a wide and deep river leading to the north, carved out of the Atlantic coast at a latitude of approximately 40° North.

Hudson investigated the river that now bears his name in September 1609, venturing as far as the present site of Albany before turning back. He had failed to find the Northwest Passage, but fifteen years later, when the Netherlands established a trading station at the mouth of the Hudson in 1624, Dutch settlers based their claims on the explorations that the English mariner had carried out while searching for China in the pay of the East India Company.

Even at the close of four decades of Dutch rule in 1664, New Amsterdam was still a small town, only 2,200 residents, and it continued to bear many of the characteristics of an isolated frontier outpost. Throughout the period, however, it had belonged to an international trading system the equal of any of its day. New Amsterdam stood on the periphery of this system. Amsterdam at its core connected the colonial port with the Orient and the rest of the world.

Details of New Amsterdam's China trade are scant.[7] Its volume must have been extremely limited, rarely more than an occasional box or crate of porcelain or silks to fill out a cargo bound for New Netherland, or a chest or two of beaver skins loaded aboard a vessel sailing for the Orient. Archaeologists who have unearthed shards of seventeenth-century Chinese porcelain in New York sites have provided some of our best evidence of the trade. We now know that at least a few of New Amsterdam's burghers used tableware imported from China. In fact, it may even be misleading to use the term "China trade" to describe commerce so intermittent and of such an inconsequential scale. Nevertheless, New Amsterdam's dealings with China were typical of colonial trading patterns and they prefigured the commerce between New York and China that would develop in the eighteenth century under British rule.

New Amsterdam's "China trade" followed an indirect course. Thanks to its government monopoly, the Dutch East India Company imported all the spices, silks, and porcelain that reached Amsterdam's markets and exported all the "specie," or silver coins, and Dutch goods that the Chinese received in return. Since a second company, the Dutch West India Company, founded in 1621, maintained a similar franchise until 1639 over commerce with the New World, for the first fifteen years after New Amsterdam's founding in 1624, pelts from the colony bound for Cathay and exotic oriental luxuries destined for the frontier town on the Hudson had to pass from one company to the other in Amsterdam. In 1639, in order to lure new settlers to New Netherland, the West India Company permitted private investors to trade between Europe and the colony.[8] Amsterdam remained the entrepôt, however, until an English fleet of four frigates carrying 400 armed men sailed into New Amsterdam harbor on September 8, 1664, captured the colony, and renamed both town and province, New York.

It is safe to assume that New Amsterdam's modest trade in China wares was among the least of the town's attractions in the eyes of its English conquerors. Since 1650, England's maritime laws had proscribed almost all direct trade between her colonies and foreign ports. Until the outbreak of the American Revolution, the Navigation Acts, which were revised on several occasions between 1650 and the mid-eighteenth century, limited commercial opportunity available to New York's merchants. Royal officials believed that a colony's proper economic role was to provide the mother country with raw materials like timber and fur, not to carry on foreign trade.

Under the English flag, New York's China trade was consequently no more direct than New Amsterdam's had been, and until the 1720s it was scarcely more active. There is no sign

Before the Revolution, Americans vehemently protested the taxes that the British government imposed on tea shipped to the colonies. Here *John Lamb* (1735–1800), a leading member of the Sons of Liberty, addresses the citizens of New York on the subject in 1774, shortly after the Boston Tea Party. A Chinese bowl that Lamb purchased after the Revolution appears in this catalogue (cat. B29 A). Illustration from Mrs. Martha Lamb and Mrs. Burton Harrison, *History of the City of New York: Its Origin, Rise and Progress* (New York, 1896) II, 763.

that New York's consumers desired oriental goods before 1720. Between the 1720s and 1750s, however, a new social custom won New York's devotion. That custom was tea drinking. Before India and Ceylon began to export the leaf in the 1830s, there was only one place to find it, China.

In 1757, the critic and wit Samuel Johnson of London described his love of tea. By his own admission, he was "a hardened and shameless Tea-drinker, who has for twenty years diluted his meals with only the infusion of this fascinating plant; whose kettle has scarcely time to cool, who with Tea amuses the evening, with Tea solaces the midnight, and with Tea welcomes the morning."[9] Johnson's devotion to tea reveals the basis of the China trade in the eighteenth century. Sometime between 1664, when an English vessel loaded a two-pound package of the leaf for its return voyage from Canton, and the early eighteenth century England became a nation of tea drinkers. Between the 1720s and the 1740s, New York and the other American colonies learned Great Britain's addiction to the steaming brew.[10]

Although her vessels carried mixed cargoes, England was building her trade with China on tea by the early eighteenth century. By the middle of the century, tea had also become the foundation of New York's China trade.[11] Like its Dutch counterpart a chartered corporation, the English East India Company held special commercial privileges, the most valuable of which was an exclusive franchise for direct trade with China. Other English merchants had to satisfy themselves with the traffic between India and China. Traveling in large fleets, the Company's lumbering cargo ships — "East Indiamen" they were called — sailed for China each year carrying silver, base metals, and textiles to exchange for huge chests packed with tea, as well as smaller shipments of porcelain, silks, and spices. In London, the Company held semiannual auctions at which it sold a portion of the tea to merchants who specialized in its export to the colonies. London's tea traders acted in turn as agents for a small group of merchants, most of them located in New York, Boston, and Philadelphia, who distributed the product throughout the colonies.[12] Other specialized merchants took responsibility for the rest of the cargo. By the early 1770s, for instance, the London firm of Hodgson and Donaldson had established an active relationship with Frederick Rhinelander of New York, a retail merchant who had developed a thriving business in Chinese and English porcelain.[13]

On the eve of the American Revolution, merchants whose businesses involved New York's China trade had favorable but limited prospects. They could look back on a half century of expanding commerce and growing opportunities. By the late 1760s, Americans imported at least 1,200,000 pounds of tea each year, of which the port of New York received several hundred thousand pounds. In fact, smugglers seeking to avoid British duties had made the city the center of an illicit trade in tea which stretched its tentacles throughout the North American colonies.[14] Meanwhile, retailers in porcelain, spices, and silks were taking advantage of New York's modest but steady demand for the luxuries that they stocked. There seemed to be no reason to foresee anything but continued prosperity. Nevertheless, the mercantile restrictions that the Navigation Acts placed on colonial merchants, prohibiting direct international trade, insured their dependence on British ports. At the end of the line connecting Canton with Great Britain's North American colonies, New York's merchants were in no position to control their own destinies. When the colonies secured their independence, these merchants would have to learn new ways to conduct their businesses.

American independence afforded New York's merchants the opportunity to test their skill and courage in international commerce, but it did not guarantee them profits. The American China trade was a perilous business in its early years, one beset by uncertainties. Competition with merchants based in American ports from Salem to Norfolk threatened sales in the Orient; competition among the merchants of South Street jeopardized profits in New York. Once trading relationships with China began to mature during the 1820s, New York's merchants could hope to predict the results of their speculations. Between 1784 and the early nineteenth century, however, each voyage was an adventure, an experiment filled with risks. What American wares would sell in China? Would the New York market welcome another cargo of tea, wicker mats, and lacquerware, or would it be glutted? What route offered the fastest and safest passage to the Orient? Would the profits repay the risks? These were the questions that worried New York's merchants, for on the answers they were wagering thousands of dollars.

The earliest voyages carried the greatest risks because they involved the greatest number of unanswered questions. When Robert Morris, Daniel Parker, William Duer, and John Holker fitted out the *Empress of China* they had no way to know whether they would be permitted to trade in Canton, or even if their vessel would be allowed to anchor in the basin at Whampoa, which the Chinese authorities had assigned to foreign cargo ships. English, French, and Chinese merchants welcomed the *Empress of China* and her supercargoes, Samuel Shaw and Thomas Randall, relieving future American traders of one worry. For each anxiety soothed, however, many more remained.

It took a special kind of man to wager a fortune on a proposition as uncertain as the China trade before the 1820s. Morris, Parker, Duer, and Holker were accustomed to large transac-

Robert Morris (1734–1806). Oil on canvas by John Wesley Jarvis after the original by Gilbert Stuart, 1817. Collection of The New-York Historical Society.

tions and substantial risks, however. They knew how to take chances, while at the same time limiting the possibility of loss.

Of the investors in the *Empress of China*, Robert Morris was the most prominent. Perhaps the wealthiest American of his day, Morris had also played a major role in winning the nation's independence. Born in England in 1734, Morris had emigrated to Maryland by the age of thirteen. After a brief period of schooling in Pennsylvania, he had taken a position in the service of the Willings of Philadelphia, a prominent family of merchants. By 1754 he had so impressed his employers with his hard work and talent that they had invited him into their firm, which assumed the name Willing, Morris & Co. The partnership's successful investments in trade, shipping, and finance made Morris wealthy and influential. Active by 1775 in the cause of independence, he received a contract from the Continental Congress to supply the American army with munitions. After service in several important positions, Morris accepted an appointment from 1781 to 1784 as Superintendent of Finance, the most powerful post under the Articles of Confederation, which governed the United States before the adoption of the Constitution.

In the course of his government service, Morris had dealt with Parker, Duer, and Holker, who were partners in a New York mercantile firm, Daniel Parker & Co., which had supplied the Continental army during the war. Each had a varied and impressive business background. Parker had traded extensively in flour. Duer had invested in naval supplies, saw mills, distilleries, and timber and was deeply involved in 1784 in the establishment of the Bank of New York. Holker, a Frenchman, had been active in shipping, privateering, land investments, and speculation in securities.[15]

Experienced businessmen like Morris, Parker, Duer, and Holker made money by taking chances. They tried their best to keep their money by minimizing their potential for loss. Diversification of cargo and division of risk were their primary strategies.

Morris, Parker, Duer, and Holker controlled their risks in the *Empress of China* in two ways. First, each limited the size of his own investment by sharing in the voyage. Second, by carrying mixed cargoes both to the Orient and home again, they reduced the possibility of weak demand for their wares either in Canton or New York. For the next four decades, New York's China traders protected themselves much as Morris and his partners had done.

The papers of the sloop *Experiment*, the second vessel to sail from New York to Canton and back, afford an insider's view of the preparations that the city's merchants made for an early voyage to China and the ways they coped with its risks. The *Experiment* had been built to carry cargo on the Hudson River, but its name was more suited to its new employment. With a displacement of only eighty tons, she was among the smallest vessels ever to test the China trade. Alongside the hulking East Indiamen, which often ran to more than 750 tons, she looked like a supply vessel. Because of her size, the *Experiment* cost substantially less to fit out than most of the other vessels venturing into Chinese waters, £11,430. Yet her investors controlled their risks as carefully as speculators in the most ambitious of voyages.

When the *Experiment* sailed past Sandy Hook at the outer opening of New York harbor in December 1785, in addition to her crew of three officers, five seamen, and two boys she carried the investments of more than twenty stockholders. The voyage's organizers had issued nineteen shares, each at a cost of £600. Eleven individuals and seven commercial partnerships had subscribed, two of the partnerships for two shares each, two of the individuals for a half share each, and each of the other investors for a share. The organizers had used this capital to assemble a varied cargo. For £15.14.0 they purchased a cask filled with the pelts of ten different species of animals, including squirrel, mink, bear, and fawn. For £49.14.0 they bought seventy-one barrels of tar. By the time they had loaded the vessel, the freight also included turpentine, rosin, tobacco, wine and spirits, ginseng, and silver dollars.

In Canton, Captain Stewart Dean sold the *Experiment*'s cargo for $7,549.50. With the receipts (which he now recorded in dollars rather than pounds) and the casks full of silver that he had brought with him, he bought tea, nankeen cloth, spices, and thirty-one chests of porcelain for his return. Eighteen months after she had sailed, the *Experiment* reentered New York harbor and the shareholders began to sell their cargo. When their sales were complete, they counted $29,820 in receipts, a profit of $16,294 after subtracting the crew's wages and the amount of their original investment.[16]

The *Experiment*'s investors had more than doubled their money in a year and a half. Such windfalls were not uncommon during the early years of the China trade, but they required both good business sense and good fortune. Most merchants who entered the China trade before the 1820s agreed that the key to success lay in good sales in Canton. If they could sell at a profit in China, they could afford the oriental luxuries for which Americans would pay dearly.

Shortly after the opening of direct commercial relations between the United States and China, Emperor Ch'ien Lung dismissed the entreaties of a British emissary for favorable trading terms with the comment that China already had everything it needed "in prolific abundance."[17] No doubt, this judgment was an exaggeration, but American merchants wondering what they could exchange at a profit in Canton must at times have nodded their heads in agreement. As large and as diverse as China was, it did indeed seem at times to have everything it needed.

Robert Morris and his partners had included ginseng, which grew wild along parts of the Hudson River, on the manifest of the *Empress of China* because colonial merchants trading via Great Britain before the American Revolution had occasionally had luck with the root.[18] Other early vessels followed Morris's example, one actually carrying thirty-eight tons of the herb,[19] but soon Canton's market became inundated with ginseng, prices fell precipitously, and demand fell short of supply. Ginseng's history in the Canton market was repeated many times over during the early years of the China trade. Knowing little about the Chinese, their needs, and tastes, American merchants relied on rumor and blind guesswork to fill their export cargoes. Such unlikely products as birds' nests and sea slugs, both for soup, and Hawaiian sandalwood for incense each experienced a brief vogue before saturating the Canton market.[20] Early China traders discovered only two exports for which there was reliable demand, silver and furs.

In China no less than in the west, silver was a precious metal used daily in commerce. The Chinese government did not mint silver coins, but in the marketplace sycee silver, broken lumps in bags, was placed on scales and traded for whatever its weight would bring. Western coins were always in demand for use as currency.

Until the early nineteenth century, silver served as the basis of western commerce to China as surely as tea was the foundation of the return trade. The precious metal was the principal American export to China as late as the late 1820s. Throughout most of the eighteenth century the English East India Company devoted fully ninety percent of the value of its export cargoes to silver;[21] as late as 1825, American exports to China included $6,524,500 in specie.[22]

Silver had an advantage in trade—the Chinese always wanted it and they were always willing to accept it. There were major disadvantages, though, the most important being that it was expensive, heavy to transport, and a temptation to pirates. In Great Britain, bullionist critics, who worried that swapping silver for tea was a bad bargain, prevented the East India Company throughout the eighteenth century from devoting even more than ninety percent of their cargoes to it. In the United States, merchants sent out vessels to Central and South America to assemble "rich cargoes," ones made up of the precious metal, for the Canton market.[23] As long as they could find nothing else to export, western merchants dealt in silver. Everyone agreed, however, that almost any other commodity would be preferable.

Before the 1820s, other than silver only furs met even a portion of the need for a commodity that Americans could provide and that the Chinese desired. Even skins, which were most in demand between 1808 and 1812, lost at least some of their attraction by the 1820s.[24]

The role that skins played in the China trade shows how complicated the search for a cargo to sell in Canton could become. The world's major fur market was in London. Here the most important dealers conducted their business. Prices for sea otter, fox, muskrat, or beaver might vary from one important fur center to another, but the London rates always affected market levels wherever pelts were traded.

American fur traders hoping to send their wares to the Orient had to keep abreast of the latest information from London, Canton, and New York, not to mention such major transshipment points for trappers in the American west as St. Louis and Detroit. The voluminous correspondence of Ramsay Crooks, general manager of the American Fur Co. from 1817 to 1834 and president thereafter until his death in 1859, reveals the complexity of this job throughout the first half of the nineteenth century. Repeated urgent letters to C. M. Lampson, with whose firm Crooks dealt in London, inquired about the latest prices there and any information about the fur trade in Canton that British merchants had gleaned.[25] Through inquiries to firms like Russell & Co., the American Fur Co.'s trading partners in Canton, Crooks tried to keep track of the most recent sales and developing opportunities.[26] Pierre Chouteau, Jr. & Co. of St. Louis[27] and William Brewster of Detroit[28] each informed Crooks of local developments in exchange for his current news about conditions in Canton. Crooks even made the difficult journey each year to the Mackinaw to make certain of his supply of skins.

Such dedication was required for success, for if there was one lesson that every China trader learned early it was that not everyone would profit in the Orient. There would be losers as well as winners. Luck was often the deciding factor in determining who would survive, but hard work laid the necessary foundation for good fortune. The success of some China traders and the failure of others ultimately transformed the commerce in two related but-distinct ways.

Between 1784 and the 1820s two contests comprised the China trade. Port competed against port for control of the commerce and merchant pitted himself against merchant for a share of his local market.

No doubt, it was fitting that on the first American voyage to the Orient the *Empress of China* had carried the hopes of not one but three major American ports: Philadelphia, where

The *General Hamilton*, built in Brooklyn in 1805, sailed to Canton in July 1806. Watercolor on paper signed "Malherbe." Alexander O. Vietor Collection, Peabody Museum of Salem. Photograph by M. W. Sexton.

Robert Morris resided; Boston, the home of supercargo Samuel Shaw; and New York, where Daniel Parker & Co. did its business. Nevertheless, however appropriate the spirit of cooperation had been, it did not last for long. Within five years, vessels from almost every Atlantic port of any consequence were testing their luck in Canton. By the end of the century, an average of ten American vessels a year sailed past Macao and up the Pearl River and merchants in Salem, Providence, Baltimore, and Norfolk were vying with those from New York, Philadelphia, and Boston for shares of the American trade in Canton.[29]

The outcome of this competition was by no means certain until the 1820s. Salem enjoyed great success for a period of two decades not only in Canton, but in the East Indies as well.[30] Providence, where the firm of Brown & Ives took an active interest in the Orient, dispatched at least seventy-nine vessels to China between 1785 and 1844, most of them before 1821.[31] At the turn of the century, Philadelphia and Boston exceeded New York both in the number of their ships in the China trade and in their size.[32] By the mid 1820s, however, New York had assumed dominance of the commerce. By 1840 even Boston's merchants were sending almost all of their cargoes from Canton to New York instead of bringing them directly home.[33] Between 1856 and 1860, New York averaged fifty arrivals each year from China, while Boston averaged only four. Only San Francisco, where thirty-three ships docked annually, most of them loaded with coolies to work for California's mining and railroad companies, could rival New York in the number of vessels it received from China.[34]

New York's control of the China trade was an aspect of a broader development, the port's growing dominance of all American foreign commerce. The symbol of New York's primacy over its rivals was the Erie Canal. Completed in 1825, the canal opened the entire Great Lakes region to trade with New York, creating an American marketplace for the city's merchants far greater than Boston, Philadelphia, Baltimore, or any other Atlantic port could match. Entrepreneurs in many cities, including Boston, Baltimore, and Philadelphia, responded by financing railroads. The technology was new, however, and New York's leadership both in foreign trade and inland commerce was already secure by the time freight cars replaced barges as the most efficient means of transporting freight between the Atlantic and the American heartland.

If the Erie Canal was the symbol of New York's leadership in foreign trade, the city's wealthiest merchants were both the prime movers and the greatest beneficiaries of this success. By the early 1830s a small group of China traders had outlasted the other competitors. With occasional additions and subtractions due to death, retirement, and failure, this circle of merchants dominated New York's China trade for years to come.

In the twentieth century, international commerce has become the preserve of large, multinational corporations which buy and sell, mine and manufacture, in countries around the globe. It is an indication of the "differentness" of the past that the great companies that we

John Jacob Astor (1763–1848). Miniature on ivory by an unidentified artist. Collection of The New-York Historical Society.

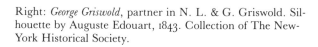

Right: *George Griswold*, partner in N. L. & G. Griswold. Sil-
houette by Auguste Edouart, 1843. Collection of The New-
York Historical Society.

Below: *South St. from Maiden Lane.* Painted and engraved
by Wm. I. Bennett, 1828. Collection of The New-York Historical Society.

take for granted today had no direct counterparts in the early nineteenth century. New York's China trade was the province of commercial partnerships and wealthy individuals.

Hundreds of men and women invested in New York's China trade between 1784 and the Civil War. There was never a time when the trade was closed to ambitious speculators with ready cash. Between the start of the nineteenth century and the mid 1820s, however, a number of individual investors battled for leadership in the commerce. Between the mid 1820s and the 1840s half a dozen mercantile partnerships competed among themselves for shares of the trade.

Of the early investors in New York's China trade, John Jacob Astor was probably the most successful; Thomas H. Smith was undoubtedly the most controversial. The sole owner of the American Fur Co. between its establishment in 1808 and 1834, Astor considered the Canton market primarily as an outlet for his pelts. Although he was especially active in the commerce before 1812, when the demand for skins was at its greatest, he continued to trade with China until the mid 1830s.[35] His estate, $20 million at his death in 1848, was the city's first great fortune built in good part on the China trade.

In contrast to Astor, Smith was New York's most spectacular loser in the China trade. A speculator of the most aggressive sort, Smith became the city's most active tea trader in the early 1820s. Relying on government regulations that allowed importers to delay payment of federal import duties for as much as eighteen months, Smith invested the money that he owed the customs collector in so much tea that he glutted the market in 1826, the price of tea dropped, and Smith went bankrupt, unable to cover $3 million in deferred tariffs.[36]

Smith's failure disrupted commerce with China for a period, but by the early 1830s equilibrium had returned. In place of the mercurial Smith, five partnerships controlled most of the trade; by the early 1840s a sixth firm, newly established, had become the most active in New York's China trade. The five original firms were N. L. & G. Griswold, Goodhue & Co., Grinnell Minturn & Co., Howland & Aspinwall, and Talbot Olyphant & Co. The sixth firm, A. A. Low & Bros., founded in 1840 by Abiel Abbot Low, who had spent the seven previous years in Canton, soon made use of his contacts and knowledge of oriental markets to become South Street's dominant China trade house.

Importers, exporters, and wholesalers, South Street's half-dozen principal China trade firms became the engines of the commerce by the 1830s. Although individuals and smaller partnerships speculated in ventures from time to time, these houses conducted the greatest share of the business. They arranged sailings, ordered shipments from their agents in Canton, and sold their cargoes to retailers at New York's auction houses. Many owned shares in the ships that carried their freight. Without the trade that they generated, there would have been no reason to sail to China.

On Course for Macao

There is hardly an experience common to modern life to compare with sailing to the Orient at the height of the China trade. No convenient analogy conveys the sights, sounds, smells, and emotions of a passage between New York and Canton. Contradictions characterized the voyage: weeks of tedium and moments of intense fear shared many a sailing, as did periods of

Right: Seal hunt on Beauchene Island, twenty leagues southeast of the Falklands. Lithograph in Edmund Fanning, *Voyages Round the World* (New York, 1838), 354.

Below: Clipper ship *Sweepstakes*. Illustration in Arthur H. Clark, *The Clipper Ship Era* (New York, 1910), 290.

homesickness and times of eager curiosity about the surprises the Orient held in store.

The voyage between New York and Canton was long, hard, and costly. It was potentially dangerous, especially in the early years when captains had to rely on general atlases like *A New System of Modern Geography* by William Guthrie rather than more appropriate maritime charts,[37] and when pirates frequently preyed on vessels loaded with silver for the Orient, forcing every vessel to travel heavily armed. The voyage kept travelers away from home for months or years, and cut them off from family letters while they were on the first leg of the journey if they sailed directly to Canton. And because markets were so unpredictable it posed financial risks. Yet in peak years, when prices for Chinese goods seemed strong and supplies appeared depleted, forty or more vessels made the passage. The attractiveness of the trade outweighed its perils.

Two principal routes linked New York and Canton, although the necessities of business might dictate any of an infinite number of variations. The most common route out of New York joined in the mid-Atlantic with the one that Portuguese navigators had plotted as early as the sixteenth century. Passing Sandy Hook, it traced a southeastern path 6,800 nautical miles long, roughly midway between the eastern coast of South America and the western shores of Africa, crossed to the south of the Cape of Good Hope, turned northeast for 5,100 nautical miles to the Sunda Strait, the channel between Java and Sumatra, then north past Borneo and Indochina to Macao, the Pearl River, and Whampoa. The second route continued along the eastern coast of South America, circled Cape Horn, then tracked north along South America's Pacific coast, usually to Valparaiso, Lima, or the western coast of North America before heading west for Canton.

The two principal routes were not significantly different in length or duration, but they held different attractions along the way. During the China trade's early, experimental period, many vessels were "transients," tramping from one port to another in search of cargoes that

Caroline Hyde Butler (1804–1892). Photograph c. 1850. Courtesy of Mrs. Thomas E. Ward.

The Island of St. Pauls. Southern Ocean. Pencil sketch in her diary by Caroline Hyde Butler, 1836. Courtesy of Mrs. Thomas E. Ward.

might sell in Canton. A voyage around the Cape of Good Hope might begin with an Atlantic crossing to Liverpool for a shipment of English textiles, or be broken in Bombay or Calcutta to take on bales of raw India cotton. The course around the southern tip of South America meant calls in Chile or Peru for silver or copper; in the Falklands, the South Shetlands, or along the coast of Oregon and Washington for furs; or in the Hawaiian Islands for sandalwood.

No matter which course a vessel set, shipboard life followed a steady routine that was punctuated only occasionally. The logs of vessels in the China trade record each crew's endless round of watches and navigational sightings. Captains took special care in shallow waters, taking frequent soundings and reminding their men to be vigilant. The Java Sea could be particularly treacherous. Until they "exchanged the green waters of the China and Java Seas for the deep blue of the Indian Ocean,"[38] many vessels like the clipper ship *Sweepstakes* dropped anchor each evening at dusk and waited until the dawn's light allowed them to proceed. When they were not standing watch or manning the sails, crewmen spent much of their time painting the ship and making repairs. "There was 3 men and the Second Mate over the starboard side a scrubbing paint and going about 8 knots," one captain recorded in his log on a December day in 1838: "Had not the men had a bowline around them they would have been washed overboard."[39]

The journal that Caroline Hyde Butler kept in 1836 and 1837 when she sailed from New York to Macao and back, aboard the ship *Roman*, provides one of the most charming and informative surviving accounts of a typical voyage to the Orient and home. Mrs. Butler, thirty-two years old at the time of her voyage, was one of a very small number of western women to see China before the middle of the nineteenth century. Threatened by consumption, she sailed with her husband, Edward, the *Roman*'s supercargo, in the hope that an ocean voyage around the Cape of Good Hope to China might strengthen her health.

Without shipboard duties of her own, Caroline Butler was free to spend the entire voyage observing everything that happened on the *Roman* and recording all that she saw. Nothing escaped her notice. Ocean-going vessels often carried livestock on deck to provide fresh meat. On her first day aboard, Caroline recorded the din that this nautical barnyard raised: "the gabbling of fowls—the quacking of ducks—the grunting of pigs—the bleating of sheep."[40] Once she reached open water, the *Roman* pitched and rolled violently. Caroline reported her feelings of malaise—"sensations I can never forget or describe."[41] In mid ocean, where days might pass in isolation from all signs of civilization, it was an event each time a crewman spied another vessel. After days without a sighting, she described the excitement of spotting the "tall masts and snowy sails" of a passing ship "in beautiful relief against the blue horizon."[42] The ocean and the skies were filled with natural wonders unlike anything that Caroline was accustomed to: whales, porpoises, sharks, and flying fish; stormy petrels, albatross, and man-o'-war birds; sunsets "varying in changing shades of gold and purple"[43] and the stars of the Magellanic Clouds, the galaxies closest to the Milky Way, "thickly studded in the blue vault of heaven."[44]

Life aboard the *Roman* required daily contact with its crew. The ship carried twenty-five men, all but two between the ages of eighteen and thirty, and one cabin boy. "Our men, with the exception of one," Caroline decided, "all possess remarkably good faces. They all appear active—good tempered and as if they would in any emergency faithfully perform their duty."

Natives attack the *Tonquin* off the coast of Washington State. Lithograph from Edmund Fanning, *Voyages to the South Seas* (New York, 1838).

One crewman, elderly and grave, Caroline nicknamed Dr. Channing "without meaning any disparagement to the great Divine," William Ellery Channing, the most eminent Unitarian minister of the day. "The other old tar," she·determined, "looks as if his head would match his clothes, a tissue of mingled *Yarns*." "I know from the very expression of his mouth and eye," Caroline added, "that he could relate many wonderful yarns relating to the awful sights he has seen at sea.... I should like to be invisible at one of this man's midnight watches and listen to his adventures with which I doubt not he nightly edifies his more youthful ship-mates."[45]

Fortunately for Caroline and the crew, except for one or two heavy gales the *Roman's* crossings were uneventful. Caroline spent many peaceful hours reading books like *Fox's Book of Martyrs*, a classic narrative of the persecutions of the early English Protestants, sketching some of the Indonesian islands that the *Roman* passed, and thinking of her home in North-ampton, Massachusetts, where she and Edward had left their four children. Holidays occa-sioned her most poignant memories. The *Roman* had sailed in October and was at sea both on Thanksgiving and Christmas. On Thanksgiving day Caroline dreamed of "my dear children — my mother, and others near and dear to me — who I know will all think of us to day, and ut-ter the sincere wish that we could set down, and partake with them of the bounties of Provi-dence."[46] The day before Christmas she wished that she "could enact the part of Santa Claus for the gratification of my dear children," but she could "very well imagine their happiness in thinking of the presents with which stockings will be filled, in the morning." "Dear little souls," she worried, "I hope they will not be disappointed!"[47]

Other ships were not as fortunate as the *Roman*. Storms, hostile natives, privateers, and an endless range of other perils each took their toll on men and vessels. In 1847 a typhoon in the Pacific nearly sank the *Houqua*, a clipper under the command of Captain Charles P. Low, A. A. Low's youngest brother. Only the captain's daring decision to lighten the *Houqua* by cutting away her masts saved her from being swamped three thousand miles from the China coast. The *Houqua* limped to her destination with a makeshift sail juryrigged from the davits for her longboat.[48] The *Eliza Gracie*, caught in a sudden gale on the last day of December 1809, lost a man overboard from the main royal yard when the storm carried away her fore top mast and main top gallant mast.[49]

The attack on the *Tonquin* by Indians provided one of the China trade's most chilling stories. Sent out in 1811 by John Jacob Astor to establish a permanent fur-trading station, Astoria, at the mouth of the Columbia River, the *Tonquin* carried thirty-three settlers and a crew of twenty-one. After depositing the settlers on the Oregon coast, she proceeded north to deal for a shipment of pelts for Canton. While in the Juan de Fuca Straits, the finger of the Pacific that separates modern-day British Columbia from the state of Washington, the *Tonquin*'s captain, a former naval officer noted for his hot temper, argued with a native chief. The following day, the chief returned with a band of warriors. Pretending to trade peacefully, the natives suddenly turned on the sailors. The *Tonquin*'s men beat off the first assault, but at the height of a second sally an explosion tore through the vessel, killing the entire crew and a large number of braves.[50]

The voyage of the *Confederacy*, sailing out of Canton for New York, ended unexpectedly in Nantes after she fell victim to a French privateer, the *Dugay-Trouin*. After almost five months at sea, the *Confederacy* was crossing the Atlantic on June 4, 1797, following calls at London and Madeira when a crewman spotted the privateer's sails to leeward. The *Dugay-Trouin* closed quickly on the *Confederacy*, unleashed two cannon shots, and although armed herself, the American vessel surrendered without resistance.[51]

Of course, most vessels managed to weather the storms they encountered; escape raiding pirates, privateers, and Indians; and complete their voyages successfully. When they sighted Macao and prepared to enter the Pearl River they entered a world largely alien to them, one unlike any other that westerners knew.

Canton

Macao was every western traveler's introduction to China. After centuries of Portuguese rule, the colony at the mouth of the Pearl River was an eccentric mixture of Orient and Occident. Nevertheless, it provided a momentary opportunity to adjust to new and strange ways before continuing on further to Canton.

From an offshore anchorage, a traveler wrote in 1829, Macao appeared "beautiful, with some romantic spots."[52] Through a telescope one could make out the governor's mansion and the Portuguese residents' houses clustered on the ridge that ran along the short peninsula on which the settlement stood. At a distance, Macao seemed a picturesque city of hills heightened by the forts and convents which capped their summits.[53] A closer examination, however, revealed a curious and contradictory community. Small gardens of great beauty relieved an unplanned and congested city. The houses of the Portuguese on the peninsula's spine rose above the densely packed huts of the Chinese.[54] By the 1820s, 50,000 people crowded into Macao's two square miles and jostled along its "narrow and irregular" streets.[55]

Of Macao's 50,000 residents, about 3,700 were European, including 2,700 women waiting for their husbands and fathers, at sea or in Canton; nearly 600 were slaves; and the rest, some 45,000, were Chinese. It was the combination of Portuguese rule and a predominantly indigenous population that gave the city its distinctive flavor. The architecture, at least the most impressive architecture, was European, much of it Iberian in style. In 1575 the Holy See had created the Roman Catholic diocese of Macao, and the Church of St. Dominic dominated one end of the city square. The crush of native Chinese in the city's treacherous streets, however, was a constant reminder that Macao was situated half a world away from Portugal. Caroline Butler was struck by the squalor of "the motley throng." "The Chinese beggars," she decided, "are I think without exception the most wretched looking objects I ever saw. New York beggars are really *kings* when *their* appearance is contrasted with these miserable beings."[56]

Although Macao's western community numbered less than 4,000, it too was curious in its composition and of only limited interest to most of the New Yorkers who were passing through. Much of the year, Macao's occidental population was almost entirely Portuguese. Its circle of English and Americans was only about thirty strong, almost all of them women. The Portuguese and their English-speaking guests had very little to do with each other, so from fall to spring between the hours of two o'clock and four the highlight of each day was the "interchange of ceremonious visits between the American and the English ladies."[57] The tedium of this routine ended in April, when the English and American merchants who had been trading in Canton left their countinghouses and retreated to Macao for the summer.

China's foreign merchant community was never very large, and a few firms controlled most of the trade. The English East India Company remained the dominant commercial force in Canton as late as the early 1830s. Its monopoly over English imports from China guaranteed the prominence of its agents, usually about a dozen in number. The Company's senior employees in Canton comprised its local policy board or "Select Committee." As long as it remained active in the China trade, by virtue of the size of its involvement in the market the Company's Select Committee acted informally as spokesman for western interests.

Although the East India Company's charter granted it a monopoly over commerce with Great Britain, the China trade's potential profits were so great that it was only a matter of time before other merchants began to look for their own niches in Canton. The East India Company's franchise did not include trade between Calcutta or Bombay and Canton, and in the 1770s British supercargoes sailing this route were the first private traders to remain in China. As resident agents they were better placed than traveling supercargoes to know market conditions and develop relationships with the merchants of the colony. After the withdrawal of the English monopoly in 1834, the two most important private houses, both British partnerships, were Jardine Matheson & Co. and Dent & Co. Each firm made its profits on the commissions that it charged for disposing of the British cargoes that it received and assembling return shipments. With rare exceptions, neither ventured its own capital in speculations.[58]

Like the private British houses, Canton's American firms grew up to replace the supercargoes who accompanied early voyages. In 1789, in fact, Samuel Shaw was the first American to make his residence in China, where he served as an agent until shortly before his death in 1794. By the 1820s and 1830s, Americans had established a half-dozen important commission firms. Each had a small staff—sometimes as few as two or three partners and several junior and senior clerks in training for partnership—and relied on friends and relatives in trading houses in New York, Boston, and the other major American ports for most of their business. None of the American firms could match Jardine Matheson & Co. or Dent & Co. in the scale of its activities. Nevertheless, the leading firms, including Russell & Co., whose partners came from Boston and New York, Olyphant & Co., whose senior partner, David W. C. Olyphant, was known for his ardent evangelical faith, and Augustine Heard & Co., founded in 1840, built lucrative businesses.[59]

Life for these western merchants followed a seasonal rhythm. The less important of their two seasons, the months from April to October, they spent in Macao with the ladies. There was very little business to transact in the Portuguese colony, so most of the hours were idle. Each October, however, they applied for permission to make the journey sixty-five miles upstream to Canton, where they spent the winter months working at a frenzied pace. There were three reasons for this seasonal pattern. Tea was a seasonal plant, which Chinese growers cultivated during the winter months in distant provinces in northern China and picked between late March and August. Chests of the leaf were not ready to ship from Canton until autumn. Nor were English or American vessels in a position to collect their cargoes until autumn, thanks to unfavorable prevailing winds during the summer. Most important of all, the merchants followed their seasonal schedule because it was what the Chinese emperor wished.

Each October, when the merchants traveled up the Pearl River, past rice fields growing green and ripe for the harvest, past the low cottages of south China's farming villages, past pagodas half hidden in groves of banyan trees,[60] they placed themselves under the authority of the Celestial Throne and the emperor's civil servants or mandarins. Each merchant's success and well-being depended on his ability to adjust to imperial law.

A quarter of a century before the voyage of the *Empress of China*, the imperial government had codified its regulations for international trade and the conduct of foreign merchants. With occasional refinements, the regulations comprising the "Canton system" remained the law of the land from 1760 until 1842.

Contemporary western merchants never really understood the Canton system or its justifications. They considered it an impractical, capricious, and restrictive welter of regulations. The mandarins, in contrast, found it a well-ordered way to do business. The Canton system was an application of the philosophical principles underlying the Chinese polity, the precepts of Confucianism.[61]

Confucian teachings addressed every aspect of life, shaping the attitudes of all who accepted them. Where governance was at issue, it taught the virtues of order and harmony. Adherents believed that a natural, hierarchical system controlled all human relationships. The emperor stood closest to heaven, the mandarins who advised him occupied a subordinate step, and by gradations the rest of mankind found their proper places still lower on the scale. The humblest rank in this order consisted of "barbarians" or *yi*. Within this category the Chinese classed the English and American merchants with whom they traded at Canton. On two oc-

Map of China. William Guthrie, *A New System of Modern Geography.* 3rd ed. (London, 1786), 663.

casions when it sent envoys to negotiate a commercial treaty with the emperor, the British government was outraged and insulted that Chinese officials would only speak with its representatives as tribute bearers from a vassal state.[62]

The mandarins found the Occidentals with whom they came in contact a strange and unpredictable people, whose puzzling customs and culture were undoubtedly inferior to China's. In their dealings with westerners the civil servants consequently aimed to control the "barbarians," regulate their behavior, and limit their contacts in China to the smallest possible number of people. One way to accomplish these goals was to restrict trade to a single open port. A second way was to establish a rigidly structured commercial system in which trustworthy Chinese merchants and other agents, acting as sureties, were always held responsible for the conduct of their trading partners. The regulations governing foreign commerce consequently had two principal provisions. First, except for the Portuguese, who traded out of Macao, and the Spaniards, who could enter at Amoy but preferred to receive cargoes by junk at Manila, western merchants could trade only in Canton. Second, except for minor items for personal use, they were required to conduct all their business in Canton through the cohong, a guild of wealthy commercial houses numbering at various times as few as four and as many as thirteen. Chinese regulations also required western merchants to hire a variety of lesser agents, including "compradors," who negotiated the provisioning and loading of vessels, and "linguists," who spoke "pidgin English," to act as interpreters.

Other regulations covered many different aspects of merchant life in Canton and the commerce that they conducted there. Vessels that proceeded up the Pearl had to pay duties, as did vessels leaving the river. The merchants were not supposed to hire personal servants, although they regularly circumvented this provision. They were not permitted to remain in Canton during the slack season or to bring their wives and daughters any farther than Macao. Nor were they or any other westerners permitted to address government representatives directly, either in person or in writing. They were required to direct petitions, marked with a Chinese superscript indicating their subservience, to the senior merchants of the cohong, who were in turn to pass these communications on to the appropriate officials.

Most galling of all, the regulations restricted western merchants to the small compound on the west bank of the Pearl where they maintained their countinghouses and quarters. Of the fifteen acres that the compound occupied, most of the area was taken up by thirteen buildings, long and narrow brick structures that faced the river. These "factories" consisted of several divisions or "houses," each separated from those in front and behind by a small courtyard. Each house contained space for a kitchen, strong room, offices, parlors, and bed chambers. Conditions in a factory's front house could be reasonably pleasant, since it commanded a view of the river and received a breeze off the water. The interior houses, in contrast, were claustrophobic and sometimes stiflingly hot.[63]

In practice, the merchants of the cohong, who were ultimately responsible to the government for the conduct of the western traders, were lax overseers who did not object to brief walks in Canton or boating excursions on the Pearl. Western merchants were not able to travel freely, however, nor deal except to a very limited degree with anyone outside the cohong. Since they could not travel to Fukien province to examine the tea crop or to Kiangsi province to consult with the porcelain makers or to Nanking to discover whether a strong year for Chinese cotton would eliminate demand for imports from India, they had to conduct much of their business by guesswork and rely on the cohong for what little news they could glean.

To function for long, the Canton system required the trust of its participants, both Occidental and Oriental. Western merchants depended on the honesty and competence of their trading partners; the members of the cohong, in turn, relied on the merchants of the factories to be responsible in their business dealings and discreet in their conduct. This mutual dependence led to many enduring relationships, the most enduring of which allied the partners of Russell & Co. with the senior merchant, Houqua.

Canton could be purgatory for western merchants, but they might console themselves with the thought that they were not in China for long. A British merchant named Thomas Beale made a fortune in Canton, went bankrupt some years later from dealing in opium, and subsequently moved to Macao, where he spent his days tending his garden and aviary. A few others like William Hunter of Russell & Co. also spent many years in China. Most of the merchants, however, agreed with Albert Heard, a partner in one of the American firms, who commented that one stayed in China only long enough to make the money to leave.[64] With skill, luck, and application, it might require less than a decade.

Abiel Abbot Low spent seven years in Canton and Macao before returning in 1840 to New York, where he opened A. A. Low & Bros., one of the premier firms in the China trade. Low's career was typical of those of many successful American merchants in the Orient in the 1830s.

Born in Salem, Massachusetts, in 1811, Low had moved to Brooklyn in 1829 when his father, Seth, an importer of drugs and India wares, had decided that New York held the future of American commerce. After working for his father for several years, Abiel had received an invitation from his father's brother, William, to join him in China. Uncle William had become a partner in Russell & Co. the same year that Seth had left Salem for Brooklyn.

Since his uncle was a partner in Russell & Co., Abiel did not have to worry whether he could find employment in Canton, but he still had to prove himself. Less fortunate men sometimes sailed for Macao without sure prospects, but with sheaves of letters of introduction to the principals of Canton's commission houses.[65] Abiel knew he could start as a junior clerk, but to win promotions he had to demonstrate to the partners his value to their firm.

As a clerk, Abiel spent four years learning his firm's business. He met the members of the cohong and developed a strong friendship with Houqua. He learned how to bargain on behalf of the agency's clients for tea and tableware, camphor and cassia, and how to find American exporters the best possible deals in China. Much of his time Abiel devoted to correspondence, often with his father, describing market conditions in Canton and requesting information on trade in other ports. After this apprenticeship, for which he received an annual salary of $500, he was ready for partnership.[66]

Abiel remained a partner of Russell & Co. for only three years, but in this short period he earned enough to secure his future. From time to time, following the advice that his father sent him, Abiel speculated successfully on his own account. His greatest earnings, however, came from his share in the profits of the firm. A clerk's salary was little more than subsistence pay in comparison to the earnings that a partner could claim. Each year between 1837 and

1840, Abiel's share of the partnership and its profits grew larger as he became more experienced and valuable to Russell & Co., and as more senior members left for home and their portions reverted to the firm. His first year, he wrote to his father in 1837, he could count on making between $8,000 and $10,000 and the following year twice as much.[67] By 1839 he estimated his annual share at $25,000.[68]

Success like Abiel's was not everyone's lot. There was not enough business to go around for every aspiring young merchant to reap profits like his. Abiel's younger brothers William and Edward each tried to copy his good fortune in the 1840s, but William could not adjust to the climate and had to return home for his health, while Edward brooded about slow promotions at Russell & Co. before winning his partnership in 1846.[69]

So many American merchants had anticipated Abiel's accomplishments, however, that the United States was already the second most important foreign trading power in China by 1810. In 1784, Great Britain, France, Holland, Denmark, Sweden, Spain, and Austria all boasted merchants in Canton when the *Empress of China* dropped anchor at Whampoa. When Abiel was a Russell & Co. partner in the late 1830s, only the British were more active in the China trade.[70] Their preeminence, however, was destined to lead to the China trade's most tragic event, the First Opium War.

Free Enterprise and the First Opium War

Although the volume of their business in China quickly surpassed that of every other western nation, Russell & Co., Olyphant & Co., and the other American houses in Canton had remained modest concerns during the 1820s and 1830s in comparison to the largest British firms. China had been an extremely profitable place for the most successful Americans to do business, but they had always recognized that the Chinese and the British had set the rules of the trade.

The Americans were bystanders, consequently, interested observers but observers nonetheless, during the China trade's most important single event, the First Opium War of 1839 through 1842, a minor military conflict with major diplomatic repercussions. Although they did not take a direct hand in the hostilities, in the end the American merchants were the beneficiaries of British pugnacity and Chinese military incompetence.

The First Opium War resulted from the convergence of three factors: a growing Chinese taste for opium that matched the west's love of tea, the development of the British textile industry, and imperial China's tradition of diplomatic hauteur. Thanks to these factors, by the mid 1830s the commercial system that the Chinese had mandated three-quarters of a century before in 1760 was no longer able to cope with the trade that the mandarins had designed it to control.

Of the three, China's growing demand for opium, abetted by the west's undoubted eagerness to supply the drug, played the central role. After decades of searching for something they could exchange for tea, western merchants began to recognize a substantial demand for opium, a demand which they nourished.

Western merchants did not introduce opium to China. Responsibility for that act rests on the shoulders of Turkish and Arab traders who were selling it in China by the end of the

OPIUM JOINTS WITH LOOKOUT ON GUARD

OPIUM STORE

PELL STREET

MOTT STREET

NEW YORK CITY.—THE OPIUM DENS IN PELL AND MOTT STREETS—HOW THE OPIUM HABIT IS DEVELOPED

FROM SKETCHES BY FRANK YEAGER.—SEE PAGE 202.

Opium Dens in New York and China

Left: *New York City—The Opium Dens in Pell and Mott Streets—How the Opium Habit is Developed.* Wood engraving after designs by Frank Yeager in *Frank Leslie's Illustrated Newspaper*, May 19, 1883, 204.

Below: *A Chinese Opium Den*, engraving by Thomas Allom in G. N. Wright, *China in a Series of Views* (1843).

seventh century or the start of the eighth. Occidental business interests did have a major role, however, in the transformation of opium from a medicine taken in small quantities to relieve pain and tension into a recreational drug used widely throughout southern China. This transformation had begun innocently enough with the introduction toward the end of the seventeenth century of the practice of smoking tobacco, which originated in America and arrived, like the rest of colonial America's exports to the Orient, indirectly by way of England and the Netherlands. To enhance their pleasure from tobacco, some smokers began to lace it with opium. By 1729, opium addiction had become enough of a social problem that the emperor, Yung-cheng, issued an injunction banning the drug's use. His order was the first in a series of edicts, each of them ineffectual, that the Chinese government promulgated over more than a century.

Until the early 1770s the opium trade remained largely in the hands of the Portuguese, who found it profitable, but a minor source of revenue. British merchants did not begin to trade extensively in the drug until 1773, when the English East India Company assumed a monopoly over Indian opium.[71] In British hands the trade became complex, lucrative, and along with tea, the basis of their oriental commerce. By the late 1830s, when Chinese authorities challenged the traffic in opium, western merchants realized that they were so dependent on the drug as a staple commodity that there would be no trade without it.

Concerned lest its participation in the traffic antagonize the Chinese government and jeopardize its access to tea, the East India Company limited its role in the developing industry to production. The most potent opium came from Benares in north-central India on the banks of the Ganges. Here by the 1830s in fields and factories under contract to the East India Company, native laborers produced thousands of chests of opium annually, each containing 120 pounds of the drug. Agricultural workers nursed the opium-bearing poppies, incised their seed capsules, and collected the gum that exuded. Other laborers dried the product, shaped it into balls weighing three or four pounds apiece, wrapped the spheres in poppy petals, and sealed them in mangowood boxes, forty per chest, for shipment to the Company auction house in Calcutta. In Calcutta, the Company sold its wares to local firms, which sent it on consignment to their correspondents in Canton, houses like Jardine Matheson & Co. and Dent & Co.[72]

The production and shipment of Indian opium fell entirely under British monopoly control, although firms in India occasionally consigned their cargoes to American houses in Canton. Every major American firm in Canton handled Indian opium except Olyphant & Co., which declined the trade due to the religious scruples of its principal partner. There was another source of opium, however, Turkey. Starting sometime around 1805, American merchants, especially from Boston but also from New York, transported the drug between the Levant and the Orient. Opium users considered the Turkish product to be of lower quality than "Benares" or "Malwa," opium from the west-central part of India, so American merchants never controlled more than a small fraction of the drug's market.[73]

Before the start of the nineteenth century, opium imports were never substantial. Until 1821, annual imports averaged no more than 4,500 chests and never exceeded 5,000. Between 1821 and 1830, however, the size of the trade doubled. By the late 1830s it had grown again to the staggering total of 40,000 chests per year. The beginnings of this growth were due ironically to the efforts of the mandarins to stamp out opium's use; the trade's later expansion had its origins in political and economic developments in London and the British north country.[74]

Despite periodic efforts to root out the opium trade, until 1820 it flourished in comparative safety in Canton, where corrupt government officials grew rich on the bribes they received in exchange for their inaction. In 1821, however, renewed efforts to control the drug forced it once and for all from the south China city. In order to escape the mandarins' unprecedented vigilance, opium dealers moved their operations from Canton to Lintin, an island in the middle of the deep-water channel at the wide entrance of the Pearl River. Here in "hulks" or old vessels permanently anchored offshore, the merchants received their illicit cargoes, paid off local officials, and distributed chests of the drug to native dealers rowing swift, many-oared "crab boats."

Before 1821, official supervision had never been effective. After 1821, almost completely out of view of the mandarins, opium sales flourished as never before. Political events in London soon encouraged even further growth.

The East India Company's monopoly of the China trade had long disturbed three wealthy and well-connected groups: the partners in Canton's private houses, who were eager to send their own cargoes directly from the Orient to London; their correspondents in London, the partners of some of Great Britain's most successful mercantile firms; and a new class of industrialists, the entrepreneurs who were building Great Britain's textile industry in cities like Manchester, and who believed that free trade with China would open an enormous and profitable market. Together, the three groups organized a campaign in the early 1830s to end the East India Company's special privileges. In 1834 they succeeded. Parliament terminated the monopoly and the Company withdrew its representatives from Canton.

Without the dominating presence of the East India Company's representatives, trade in Canton became a free-for-all matching established private firms against each other and newcomers. Meanwhile, in the Pearl River off Lintin the flood of opium swelled, prices rose and fell wildly, and worried opium dealers began to order their trading ships to cruise the China coast in search of new customers.

At first, Chinese civil servants were uncertain how to respond to the opium trade's explosive growth. Efforts over more than a century to control the business had been so ineffectual that some mandarins proposed the drug's legalization. Western merchants were encouraged in 1836 when they received word of a report to the emperor by Hsü Nai-chi, an officer of the Court of Sacrificial Worship. Hsü acknowledged the pernicious effects of opium, but argued that even the government's best efforts to eradicate the black-market industry would inevitably fail. Hsü's memorial was the most comprehensive statement in a brief movement to end sanctions against the drug. By 1837, however, the emperor had come to another conclusion. He would redouble surveillance and end the traffic once and for all.[75]

The effects of renewed efforts to stamp out opium became apparent almost immediately. Within months, western traders in Canton were complaining that the emperor's policies had intimidated the natives and caused stagnation in their markets.[76] International economic difficulties reaching into various western nations and felt in the United States in the form of a financial collapse and depression, the "Panic of 1837," briefly conspired with imperial efforts to bring commerce in Canton to a standstill. By the end of 1838, however, it was becoming clear to Chinese authorities that their program to seal off China from "foreign mud" required the concentrated attention of one of their most able administrators.

The emperor's choice was Lin Tse-hsü, governor-general of the Hu-Kuang region, which was comprised of Hupeh and Hunan provinces, and one of China's most trusted and capable officials. As a young man Lin had progressed rapidly from post to post within the government, each time repaying the faith that his superiors and the emperor had placed in him with an outstanding performance. On several occasions in the 1820s he had served as a problem solver for the emperor, taking on positions of greater responsibility than able men ten years his senior held. In 1838 Lin was fifty-three years old, corpulent, and troubled by health difficulties.[77]

There can be no doubt that Commissioner Lin was an astute and capable official. In fact, by contemporary standards his was among China's most moderate and progressive voices. A scholar-administrator, like all mandarins, Lin devoted much of his attention to methods of modernizing Confucian teachings to accommodate China's changing social and economic circumstances. As a product of a demanding and rigid system of education and examinations, however, Lin remained committed to its basic tenets. His attitudes concerning the relationship of the Celestial Throne with foreign governments allowed no room for flexibility.

In response to Hsü Nai-chi's proposal in 1836 to legalize opium dealings, Lin had prepared a vigorous rejoinder. In a six-point plan he had proposed to concentrate on reforming native addicts, punishing native dealers, and avoiding, for the present, bringing pressure on foreign merchants.[78] It would be impossible, however, to deal with Chinese involvement in the trade without also challenging western interests.

Lin arrived in Canton on March 10, 1839. Eight days later he issued his first proclamations. There would be no negotiating with foreign merchants, no placating them, no attention to the needs of their trade. Within three days they would turn over all the opium in their possession and sign bonds pledging never to import the drug again. The commissioner stopped all trade, blockaded the western factories, and ordered the western merchants' Chinese domestics to leave their employers immediately.

Lin's edict posed a serious threat to western commerce and to the mercantile community residing in Canton's factories, but led by the British the traders refused at first to reply. After decades of rebuffs by the emperor whenever they attempted to establish their equality in diplomatic and commercial relations, the British resisted what they considered to be Lin's bullying. Surrounded in their compound by Chinese troops, unable to conduct business, the merchants spent a week in close confinement before Captain Charles Elliot, the senior British government official on the scene, ordered the firms to turn more than 20,000 chests of opium over to Lin, then leave Canton immediately. Of the opium covered by Elliot's order, Americans held 1,540 chests on consignment from British trading houses in India.[79]

When the British withdrew from Canton, they left the American merchant community behind. Never as concerned about the niceties of diplomacy as the British, nor as dependent on the opium trade, the Americans were willing to do whatever was necessary to remain in business. At home in New York by 1840, A. A. Low applauded the decision to continue in residence in Canton, and reported that most Americans sympathized with the Chinese.[80] Even British merchants, who now took up positions on ships off Hong Kong, were supportive when they discovered that they could resume their trade by paying American firms like Russell & Co. a service charge to clear their cargoes through Chinese customs and freight them down the Pearl River to international waters.

The situation was unstable, but deliberations in London promised a resolution. By November 1839 Prime Minister Palmerston, bowing to the heavy lobbying efforts of the China trade merchants of London and Liverpool, ordered an expeditionary force to sail for China. Charged with the responsibility of restoring British prestige and winning diplomatic recognition from the Chinese, the force of sixteen vessels arrived in June 1840 and blockaded the entrance to the Pearl. The First Opium War was underway.

The First Opium War was a brief affair, bloody at times, but often little more than a series of minor skirmishes. The outcome was never in question. Antique Chinese forts and war junks were no match for the broadsides of the pride of the British navy, nor could Chinese troops stand up to highly trained British regiments. After intermittent fighting both on land and sea, the Chinese sued for peace, and in Nanking on August 29, 1842, the two nations signed the treaty that ended hostilities.

Of minor significance as a military conflict, the First Opium War had far more substantial implications for diplomacy and international commerce. British merchants and emissaries had objected for decades to the maddeningly supercilious nature of Chinese officials, the apparent capriciousness of Chinese law, and the frustrating constraints under which traders had to conduct their business. Whether or not these complaints were justified, the British, as the victors, were in position to impose a settlement. The terms they secured at Nanking served as the model two years later for the Treaty of Wanghia between the United States and the Celestial Empire and as the basis of relations between China and the west until the outbreak of the Second Opium War in 1856.

Although the treaties of Nanking and Wanghia differed in many of their particulars and emphases, most of their principal provisions were very similar. Each treaty opened four new ports to western trade: Foochow, Ningpo, Amoy, and Shanghai. Each guaranteed the principle of extraterritoriality—neither British nor American citizens were to be subject to Chinese criminal law, but would be governed by the laws of their own nations. And by signing the treaties the Chinese recognized Great Britain and the United States as equals rather than subordinate or vassal states. In addition, the Treaty of Nanking ceded control of Hong Kong to the British and dissolved the cohong in Canton.

Now that China was opening up to the west, New York's merchants had to take advantage of their new opportunities. As Chinese and American diplomats were signing the Treaty of Wanghia, on the ocean between New York and the Orient, the China trade's climactic day was already dawning, the day of the clipper ship.

Clipper Ship Days

They were the perfection of the shipbuilder's art and craft. Their finest days coincided with the zenith of New York's China trade. *Flying Cloud... Sea Witch... Typhoon:* their names sang of their power, their speed, and their grace. They epitomized all that the China trade had

The *Rainbow*. From a drawing
by Worden Wood, 1918. Photograph, collection of The
New-York Historical Society.

promised. Yet they also warned of the end of an era. By the late 1850s the old China trade
passed from the scene, replaced by new interests and new ways of doing business.

If ever a vessel was designed for a specific role it was the China clipper. China traders
had always welcomed speed and carrying capacity, but in the early years the uncertainty of
markets in New York and Canton had encouraged them to invest in craft of modest size and
cost. The need, moreover, to search for cargoes in Europe, along the South American coast,
in the Falklands, the Oregon territory, or the Hawaiian Islands which the Chinese would accept in exchange for their tea and other wares retarded voyages and reduced the advantage
that fast vessels held over slower ones. By the 1830s, though, as commerce and competition
became more and more spirited, ships in the China trade began to grow noticeably larger
and faster than they had been. By the early 1840s they began to assume the exaggerated lines
that characterized the classic China clipper.[81]

What made a ship a clipper? True clippers were massive vessels, far larger than the 300-
or 400-ton ships that John Jacob Astor and Thomas H. Smith had sent out early in the nineteenth century, to say nothing of the 80-ton *Experiment*. Even the smallest clippers displaced
nearly 500 tons and among the most famous, the *Sea Witch* was rated at 890 tons, the *N. B.
Palmer* at 1,490 tons, and the *Flying Cloud* at 1,793 tons. A few clippers exceeded 2,000 tons, and
one, the *Great Republic*, stood at more than 3,000 tons, although she never carried a cargo as
far as China. It might seem that size would retard speed, but not in the case of the clippers.
Naval architects like Donald McKay of Massachusetts, who constructed many of the grandest of the clippers, built them concave-bowed rather than bluff-bowed, with a long and lean
line forward which widened to its greatest breadth farther aft than in traditional designs. Aloft,
they carried strengthened masts and yards in order to set far more sail than had previously
been customary.

If the winds were right, sleek lines and billowing clouds of sail allowed the clippers to race across the oceans at greater speeds than even the steamships could make before the twentieth century, sometimes more than twenty knots. When they were new, before their live-oak boards absorbed seawater and became weighted down, the fastest of the clippers were able to complete the voyage to China and back in less than half the fifteen months that the *Empress of China* had required. By the early 1850s, a crossing one way of less than one hundred days, while still considered fast, was no longer exceptional. The record time for a single crossing, seventy-seven days in 1848 by the *Sea Witch* under the command of Captain Robert Waterman, was fifty-eight days faster than the *Empress of China*'s passage from Canton to New York in 1785.

The ancestry of the clipper ship reached back to eighteenth-century French naval frigates and daring Maryland privateers, known as "Baltimore clippers," built to fight in the War of 1812. The first China clipper, however, was the *Ann McKim*, which was launched in Baltimore in 1832. At 493 tons she was large for her day, but only a suggestion of the size and extreme lines of the vessels that would follow her. Isaac McKim, a Baltimore merchant, built and owned her for five years, until his death in 1837. When the firm of Howland & Aspinwall purchased her from McKim's estate, she became New York's first China clipper.[82]

Wary shipbuilders were slow to copy the *Ann McKim*. Seven years elapsed between her construction and the launching of the next clipper, the 650-ton *Akbar*, in 1839. When the *Akbar* made her first crossing to Canton in 109 days, however, at the time a very rapid passage, skeptics were quick to notice. Other vessels soon followed the *Akbar* down the ways, larger with each passing year and more daring in their design. By 1845, when Howland & Aspinwall launched the *Rainbow*, with a displacement of 750 tons and a bow so sharp that some observers questioned whether she could sail properly, naval architects had finally arrived at the classic clipper ship.

As they sped between New York and the Orient, the clippers raced with an adolescent's energy. Their youthful vigor belied their roles as heralds, however, of a new and different China trade.

In its infancy it was fear of risk that had characterized the China trade and shaped the commercial practices of its merchants. Fear of maritime disasters had induced competitors to cooperate on voyages, each thereby limiting his risk on a given venture. Fear of fickle markets had encouraged them to control their risks by sending mixed cargoes to the Orient and ordering diversified return shipments through their agents in Canton. There were always risks in trade, in the 1850s as well as the 1790s. Experience taught prudent merchants about the chances they were taking, however, and showed them how to take their risks into account. By the height of the clipper ship era, New York's China merchants had learned their business, and the China trade had settled into a new routine.

Three traits distinguished the China trade in the late 1840s and early 1850s from the same commerce at the start of the century: concentration in a single port, New York; concentration on a single commodity for each major leg of the trade, Turkish and Indian opium for voyages to the Orient, tea on the return home; and concentration of the trade in the hands of a small number of wealthy investors. We have already seen how each of these developments began. New York asserted its supremacy over the China trade in the 1820s. Tea and opium had become its staples by the 1830s. Half a dozen New York firms, including Grinnell Minturn &

Co., Howland & Aspinwall, and A. A. Low & Bros. took control of the trade between the early 1830s and the early 1840s.

By the mid 1840s the rise of the clipper ships marked the culmination of the concentration of the China trade in a few wealthy hands. Clippers were expensive to build and fit out. In 1832 Isaac McKim had stinted no cost when he had constructed the *Ann McKim*. She was a beautiful vessel, her fittings of Spanish mahogany and brass. McKim's example had set the tone for future clippers. Each entailed a major investment. The *Houqua*, which a New York shipyard, Brown & Bell, built in 1844, required $45,000 to ready for her first voyage. Five years later in 1849 the *Oriental* cost $70,000. These were enormous sums at the time. Yet in contrast to the *Experiment*, which had been owned by more than twenty shareholders, the clippers were owned by individual mercantile houses.

Sole ownership entailed risks, but prudent investors now recognized that these chances were worth taking. Mercantile firms like A. A. Low & Bros., which owned sixteen clippers at various times,[83] and Howland & Aspinwall built large fleets of the elegant vessels. The greatest profits, they had learned, were not in trade at all, but in shipping. Despite their enormous costs, clippers could achieve such great speeds that their owners could charge far more for freight than more traditional cargo haulers could command. In Hong Kong in 1850, Russell & Co. chartered the *Oriental* at £6 per ton for a shipment of tea to London, while slower British vessels waited at anchor high in the water, unable to fill their holds at £3.10 per ton. At such high rates, many clippers paid off their initial costs in a single voyage.[84]

When mercantile houses like Howland & Aspinwall and A. A. Low & Bros. began to concentrate on shipping rather than commerce, the end drew near for the old China trade.

Advertisement for the Great American Tea Company. Engraving, 1863. Bella C. Landauer Collection, The New-York Historical Society.

Canton and the promise of the China trade had lured Samuel Shaw, Thomas Smith, A. A. Low, and countless others, encouraging them to take a chance for the sake of a possible profit. Now, Low and the others thought neither of China nor of the trade. As shippers, these old China traders now sent their vessels wherever they could find a cargo to haul at a rate that would pay. Forty-niners bound for the gold fields of California would pay premium prices; San Francisco commanded the shippers' attention in the early 1850s. Another gold rush, this one in Australia, turned all eyes to Melbourne in 1851. Although they did not ignore their old haunts in Macao, Whampoa, and Canton, or Hong Kong, China's new center for import and export, there were other ports and other projects in their future.

1. Later vessels were able to cut thousands of miles off the course that the *Empress of China* followed, reducing the round trip to approximately 26,000 miles. First-person accounts of the voyage appear in Josiah Quincy, ed., *The Journals of Major Samuel Shaw, the First American Consul at Canton* (Boston, 1847), 131–213, and "Letters Relating to the Trade with China" in Arthur Harrison Cole, ed., *Industrial and Commercial Correspondence of Alexander Hamilton, Anticipating his Report on Manufactures* (Chicago, 1928), 129–161. Useful secondary accounts include Foster Rhea Dulles, *The Old China Trade* (Boston, 1930), 1–12, and Clarence L. ver Steeg, "Financing and Outfitting the First United States Ship to China," *Pacific Historical Review*, XXII (1953), 1–12.

2. Quincy, ed., *Journals of Major Samuel Shaw*, 218.

3. *Loudon's New-York Packet*, May 12, 1785.

4. Dulles, *Old China Trade*, 49.

5. *Pennsylvania Packet*, May 16, 1785.

6. On Dutch trade in the sixteenth and seventeenth centuries, see Ralph Davis, *The Rise of the Atlantic Economies* (Ithaca, 1973), 176–193.

7. For a brief account of New Netherland's China trade, see Jean McClure Mudge, *Chinese Export Porcelain for the American Trade, 1785–1835* (Newark, 1962), 63–66.

8. Thomas J. Condon, *New York Beginnings: The Commercial Origins of New Netherland* (New York, 1968).

9. Quoted in Benjamin Woods Labaree, *The Boston Tea Party* (London, 1966), 3.

10. Labaree, *Boston Tea Party*, 3–14.

11. Labaree, *Boston Tea Party*, 3–14.

12. Labaree, *Boston Tea Party*, 5.

13. See Day Book, 1772–1774; Day Book, 1774–1777; Order Book, 1772–1774, Frederick Rhinelander Papers, New-York Historical Society.

14. Labaree, *Boston Tea Party*, 12.

15. ver Steeg, "Financing and Outfitting," *Pacific Historical Review*, XXII (1953), 3–4.

16. Papers of the sloop *Experiment*, New-York Historical Society.

17. Quoted in James C. Thomson, Jr., et al., *Sentimental Imperialists: The American Experience in East Asia* (New York, 1981), 31.

18. Dulles, *Old China Trade*, 6.

19. Henry Lee, "The Magee Family and the Origins of the China Trade," Massachusetts Historical Society, *Proceedings*, LXXXI, 107.

20. Thomson, et al., *Sentimental Imperialists*, 32.

21. Michael Greenberg, *British Trade and the Opening of China, 1800–42* (New York, 1951), 6–7.

22. Greenberg, *British Trade*, 219.

23. Greenberg, *British Trade*, 8.

24. Greenberg, *British Trade*, 88.

25. C. M. Lampson to Ramsay Crooks, Esq., London, July 4, 1838, American Fur Co. Papers, New-York Historical Society.

26. Russell, Sturgis & Co. to Ramsay Crooks, Esq., Canton, August 1, 1838, American Fur Co. Papers, New-York Historical Society.

27. American Fur Co. to Pierre Chouteau, Jr. & Co., New York, April 16, 1842, American Fur Co. Papers, New-York Historical Society.

28. William Brewster to Ramsay Crooks, Esq., Detroit, Dec. 28, 1837, American Fur Co. Papers, New-York Historical Society.

29. Dulles, *Old China Trade*, 106.

30. Dulles, *Old China Trade*, 29.

31. James B. Hedges, *The Browns of Providence Plantations: The Nineteenth Century* (Providence, 1968), 17–25, 89–104, 121–124, 136–142, 148–152.

32. Lawrence H. Leder, "American Trade to China, 1800–1802: Some Statistical Notes," *American Neptune*, XXIII (1963), 215.

33. Samuel Eliot Morison, *The Maritime History of Massachusetts, 1783–1860* (Cambridge, 1921), 275.

34. Robert Greenhalgh Albion, *The Rise of New York Port, 1815–1860* (New York, 1939), 203.

35. *Shipping and Commercial List and New-York Price Current*, June 21, 1834.

36. Mudge, *Chinese Export Porcelain*, 94; Albion, *Rise of New York Port*, 198.

37. Dulles, *Old China Trade*, 35–36.

38. Notes of a Voyage from Shanghai to New York in [the] Clipper Ship *Sweepstakes*, Dec. 28, 1856, New-York Historical Society.

39. Logbook of an unidentified sailing ship, kept on a voyage from Canton to New York, Dec. 6, 1838, New-York Historical Society.

40. Caroline Hyde Butler, Journal of a Voyage to China in the Year 1836–7 on the Ship *Roman*, Capt. Benson. Unpublished manuscript in private possession, Oct. 11, 1836.

41. Butler, Journal, Oct. 11, 1836.

42. Butler, Journal, Dec. 15, 1836.

43. Butler, Journal, Dec. 17, 1836.

44. Butler, Journal, Jan. 7, 1837.

45. Butler, Journal, Nov. 5, 1836.

46. Butler, Journal, Dec. 1, 1836.

47. Butler, Journal, Dec. 24, 1836.

48. Helen Augur, *Tall Ships to Cathay* (Garden City, 1951), 162–177.

49. Journal of a Voyage from Canton to New York in the Ship *Eliza Gracie*, Dec. 31, 1809, New-York Historical Society.

50. Dulles, *Old China Trade*, 62–63.

51. Notes from the *Confederacy* Log [transcription], June 4–9, 1797, New-York Historical Society.

52. "Harriet Low's Journal 1829–1834" in Elma Loines, ed., *The China Trade Post-Bag of the Seth Low Family of Salem and New York* (Manchester, Maine, 1953), III.

53. Butler, Journal, essay on "The Penha."

54. Greenberg, *British Trade*, 132.

55. Loines, *China Trade Post-Bag*, III.

56. Butler, Journal, Feb. 18, 1837.

57. Butler, Journal, essay on "Life of Foreign Ladies at Macoa [sic]."

58. Greenberg, *British Trade*, 18–40.

59. Dulles, *Old China Trade*, 123.

60. Rev. William A. Macy to William A. Butler, Canton, Nov. 1856, Butler Family Papers, New-York Historical Society.

61. Thomson, et al., *Sentimental Imperialists*, 21–22.

62. Jean Chesneaux, et al., *China from the Opium Wars to the 1911 Revolution* (New York, 1976), 4–13.

63. Peter Ward Fay, *The Opium War, 1840–42* (Chapel Hill, 1975), 19–21.

64. Thomson, et al., *Sentimental Imperialists*, 38.

65. For example, see the following letters of introduction on behalf of A. A. Low's brother, Edward: R. B. Forbes to Messrs. Russell & Co., Boston, Nov. 8, 1841; A. A. Low to [illeg.] Gilman, New York, Nov. 11, 1841; A. A. Low to Edward King, New York, Nov. 13, 1841; A. A. Low to W. Delano, Jr., Esq., New York, Nov. 15, 1841; A. A. Low to Augustine Heard & Co., New York, Nov. 15, 1841; A. A. Low to Messrs. Russell & Co., New York, Nov. 15, 1841,

A. A. Low Letterbook, Low Family Papers, New-York Historical Society.

66. Augur, *Tall Ships to Cathay,* 82.

67. A. A. Low to Seth Low, Canton, July 10, 1837, A. A. Low Letterbook, Low Family Papers, New-York Historical Society.

68. A. A. Low to Seth Low, Canton, Jan. 2, 1839, A. A. Low Letterbook, Low Family Papers, New-York Historical Society.

69. Augur, *Tall Ships to Cathay*, 158.

70. Dulles, *Old China Trade*, 17, 106.

71. Greenberg, *British Trade*, 105.

72. Fay, *Opium War*, 3–14.

73. Charles C. Stelle, "American Trade in Opium to China, Prior to 1820," *Pacific Historical Review*, IX (1940), 425–444; Stelle, "American Trade in Opium to China, 1821–39," *Pacific Historical Review*, X (1941), 57–74.

74. Greenberg, *British Trade*, 221.

75. Hsin-pao Chang, *Commissioner Lin and the Opium War* (Cambridge, 1964), 85–92.

76. Greenberg, *British Trade*, 199.

77. Chang, *Commissioner Lin*, 120–131; Fay, *Opium War*, 128–129.

78. Chang, *Commissioner Lin*, 93.

79. Dulles, *Old China Trade*, 156.

80. A. A. Low to R. B. Forbes, Esq., Canton, Nov. 9, 1840, A. A. Low Letterbook, Low Family Papers, New-York Historical Society.

81. Arthur H. Clark, *The Clipper Ship Era* (New York, 1910).

82. Clark, *Clipper Ship Era*, 57–72.

83. William G. Low, *A. A. Low & Brothers' Fleet of Clipper Ships*, 2nd ed., (n.p., 1922).

84. Clark, *Clipper Ship Era*, 97–98, 104.

Manuscript Sources

Unless otherwise noted, collections are located in The
New-York Historical Society.

American Fur Co. papers.

Butler Family papers.

Butler, Caroline. Journal of a voyage to China in the year
1836-7 on the ship *Roman*, Capt. Benson. In the private possession of Mrs. Thomas E. Ward.

Chrystie, Mary. Receipt book, 1801-1806.

William Duer papers.

Experiment papers.

Admiral C. F. Goodrich papers.

Iselin, Isaac. Voyage on the *Maryland*.

Journal of a voyage from Canton to New York in the ship
Eliza Gracie.

Journal of the voyage of the ship *Edward* to Canton, 1829-
1830.

Journal of the voyage of the ship *Sarah Snow*.

Logbook of an unidentified ship, 1838.

Logbook of the ship *Confederacy*.

Logbook of the ship *Helena*.

Low Family papers.

Notes of a voyage from Shanghai to New York in the clipper ship *Sweepstakes*.

Frederick Rhinelander papers.

United States of America. Port of New-York. List of officers and men comprising the crew of the ship *South
Carolina*.

Oliver Walcott & Co. papers.

Printed Sources

Albion, Robert Greenhalgh. *The Rise of New York Port, 1815-
1860*. New York: Charles Scriber's Sons, 1939.

Augur, Helen. *Tall Ships to Cathay*. Garden City, New York:
Doubleday & Company, Inc., 1951.

Bachman, Van Cleaf. *Peltries or Plantations: The Economic
Policies of the Dutch West India Company in New Netherland, 1623-1639*. Baltimore: Johns Hopkins University Press, 1969.

Barbour, Violet. *Capitalism in Amsterdam in the Seventeenth
Century*. Baltimore: The Johns Hopkins University
Press, 1950.

Beeching, Jack. *The Chinese Opium Wars*. New York: Har-
court Brace Jovanovich, 1975.

Bjork, Gordon C. "The Weaning of the American Economy: Independence, Market Changes, and Economic Development." *Journal of Economic History* 24:
541-566.

Chang, Hsin-pao. *Commissioner Lin and the Opium War*.
Cambridge, Mass.: Harvard University Press, 1964.

Chernow, Barbara A. "Robert Morris and Alexander
Hamilton: Two Financiers in New York." In *Busi-
ness Enterprise in Early New York*, edited by Joseph R.
Frese, S.J., and Jacob Judd. Tarrytown: Sleepy
Hollow Press, 1979.

Chesneaux, Jean; Bastide, Marianne; and Bergère, Marie-
Claire. *China from the Opium Wars to the 1911 Revolution*. New York: Pantheon Books, 1976.

Clark, Arthur H. *The Clipper Ship Era*. New York: G. P.
Putnam's Sons, 1910.

Cole, Arthur Harrison, ed. *Industrial and Commercial Correspondence of Alexander Hamilton Anticipating his Report
on Manufactures*. Chicago: A. W. Shaw Company,
1928.

Condon, Thomas J. *New York Beginnings: The Commercial
Origins of New Netherland*. New York: New York University Press, 1968.

Davis, Ralph. *The Rise of the Atlantic Economies*. Ithaca:
Cornell University Press, 1973.

Dennett, Tyler. *Americans in Eastern Asia: A Critical Study of
the Policy of the United States with reference to China, Japan and Korea in the 19th Century*. New York: MacMil-
lan Company, 1922.

Downs, Jacques M. "A Study in Failure—Hon. Samuel
Snow." *Rhode Island History* 25: 1-8.

Dulles, Foster Rhea. *China and America: The Story of their Relations Since 1784*. Princeton: Princeton University
Press, 1946.

————. *The Old China Trade*. Boston: Houghton Mifflin
Company, 1930.

East, Robert A. *Business Enterprise in the American Revolutionary Era*. New York: Columbia University Press,
1938.

Fairbank, John King. *Trade and Diplomacy on the China Coast:
The Opening of the Treaty Ports, 1842-1854*. Stanford:
Stanford University Press, 1973.

————. *The United States and China*. 4th ed. Cambridge,
Mass.: Harvard University Press, 1979.

Fanning, Edmund. *Voyages Around the World*. New York,
1838.

————. *Voyages to the South Seas, Indian and Pacific Oceans*. 5th
ed. New York, 1838.

Fay, Peter Ward. *The Opium War, 1840-1842*. Chapel Hill:
University of North Carolina Press, 1975.

Goldstein, Jonathan. *Philadelphia and the China Trade, 1682-
1846: Commercial, Cultural, and Attitudinal Effects*. University Park: Pennsylvania State University Press, 1978.

Greenberg, Michael. *British Trade and the Opening of China,
1800-1842*. Cambridge, Eng.: Cambridge University Press, 1951.

Griffin, Eldon. *Clippers and Consuls: American Consular and*

Commercial Relations with Eastern Asia, 1845-1860.
Ann Arbor: Edwards Brothers, Inc. 1938.

Hanyan, Craig R. "China and the Erie Canal." *Business History Review* 35: 558-566.

Harrington, Virginia D. *The New York Merchant on the Eve of the Revolution.* New York: Columbia University Press, 1935.

Hedges, James B. *The Browns of Providence Plantations: The Nineteenth Century.* Providence: Brown University Press, 1968.

Hunter, William C. *Bits of Old China.* London, 1885.

———. *The "Fan Kwae" at Canton before Treaty Days, 1825-1844.* 2nd ed. Shanghai, 1911.

Johnston, Henry P. *The Correspondence and Public Papers of John Jay.* Vol. III. New York: G. P. Putnam's Sons, 1891.

Labaree, Benjamin Woods. *The Boston Tea Party.* London: Oxford University Press, 1966.

Leder, Lawrence H. "American Trade to China, 1800-1802: Some Statistical Notes." *American Neptune* 23: 212-218.

Lee, Henry. "The Magee Family and the Origins of the China Trade." Massachusetts Historical Society, *Proceedings* 81: 104-119.

Loines, Elma, ed. *The China Trade Post-Bag of the Seth Low Family of Salem and New York, 1829-1873.* Manchester, Maine: Falmouth Publishing House, 1953.

Liu, Kwang-Ching. *Americans and Chinese: A Historical Essay and a Bibliography.* Cambridge, Massachusetts: Harvard University Press, 1963.

Low, William G. *A. A. Low & Brothers' Fleet of Clipper Ships.* 2nd ed. N.p., 1922.

Luke, Myron H. *The Port of New York, 1800-1810: The Foreign Trade and Business Community.* New York, 1953.

Miller, Stuart Creighton. *The Unwelcome Immigrant: The American Image of the Chinese, 1785-1882.* Berkeley and Los Angeles: University of California Press, 1969.

Morison, Samuel Eliot. *The Maritime History of Massachusetts, 1783-1860.* Boston: Houghton Mifflin Company, 1921.

Mudge, Jean McClure. *Chinese Export Porcelain for the American Trade, 1785-1835.* Newark: University of Delaware Press, 1962.

Porter, Kenneth Wiggins. *John Jacob Astor, Business Man.* 2 vols. Cambridge, Mass.: Harvard University Press, 1931.

Putnam, Alfred P. *A Noble Life: A Discourse Commemorative of Abiel Abbot Low.* Boston, 1893.

Quincy, Josiah, ed. *The Journals of Major Samuel Shaw, the First American Consul at Canton.* Boston, 1847.

Slaughter, Thomas Paul. "The American Vision of China, 1784-1806: European and American Merchant-Consul Influences." Honors thesis, University of Maryland, 1976.

Smith, George L. *Religion and Trade in New Netherland: Dutch Origins and American Development.* Ithaca: Cornell University Press, 1973.

Spann, Edward K. *The New Metropolis: New York City, 1840-1857.* New York: Columbia University Press, 1981.

Stelle, Charles C. "American Trade in Opium to China, Prior to 1820." *Pacific Historical Review* 9: 425-444.

——— "American Trade in Opium to China, 1821-39." *Pacific Historical Review* 10: 57-74.

Sterling, David L. "William Duer, John Pintard, and the Panic of 1792." In *Business Enterprise in Early New York*, edited by Joseph R. Frese, S. J., and Jacob Judd. Tarrytown: Sleepy Hollow Press, 1979.

Thomson, James C., Jr.; Stanley, Peter W.; and Perry, John Curtis. *The Sentimental Imperialists.* New York: Harper & Row, 1981.

Ver Steeg, Clarence L. "Financing and Outfitting the First United States Ship to China." *Pacific Historical Review* 22: 1-12.

Wallerstein, Immanuel. *The Modern World-System II: Mercantilism and the Consolidation of the European World-Economy, 1600-1750.* New York: Academic Press, 1980.

Ward, Edith Nevill Smythe, ed. *A Family Heritage: Letters and Journals of Caroline Hyde Butler Laing, 1804-1892.* East Orange, N.J.: [privately printed], 1957.

Wilbur, Marguerite Eyer. *The East India Company and the British Empire in the Far East.* New York: Richard R. Smith, 1945.

Wilkenfeld, Bruce M. "The New York City Shipowning Community, 1715-1764." *American Neptune* 37: 50-65.

Catalogue of the Exhibition

Catalogue Introduction

An exhibition catalogue serves two main purposes. It is an aid to those who are able to visit the exhibition and it is a permanent record both for those who have visited and those who were unable to do so.

While this catalogue is no exception, it is fortunate in being able to break new ground, for the links between New York and China have never been well illustrated and a great many of the items exhibited are emerging for the first time as objects of historical interest. Indeed, had this exhibition taken place as recently as twenty-five years ago, the majority of exhibits would still have been in the hands of the families for whom they were made.

In spite of the assembling of some three hundred diverse objects, mostly porcelain, the organizers are far more aware now than they were a year ago of the great volume of pieces which will *not* be shown. Some are recorded but may never be found. One wonders for instance what became of some orders for the second voyage of the *Empress of China* in 1786:

"A table sett Nankin Blue and White China, 170 pieces marked I.W.N."

or

"A tea sett China for Mrs. Wilkinson"

or yet again

"A sett of Mother of Pearl Counters for Mrs. Bunner."

It was of course the chance of profit that kept the trade going. Robert Morris, the principal financier of the *Empress of China*, wrote to John Jay (cat. c52) that its owners hoped "to encourage others in the adventurous pursuit of commerce." But it was the excitement caused by the charm, originality, and quality of the goods which kept it going so long.

The trading patterns of the seventeenth century, revealed in the excavations of shards in upstate New York, give way to the steady growth of trading in the early and mid eighteenth century from which a number of whole pieces survive.

It is a matter of some regret that it has not been possible to make more use of the massive records contained in the Rhinelander papers, now so carefully worked through by Mrs. Arlene Schwind.

The will of Margaret Van Varick in Albany in 1695/6 mentions East India silver, "1 Jappon wooden dish," "1 China cupp bound with silver," and a great many other pieces of china, including "basens and jugs," "2 East India floure potts white," and "1 Lyon."

The "Appraisment" of the estate of Brandt Schuyler of New York between 1730 and 1762 includes "6 Burnt China cordial cups whereof 2 are broke. . ." (we do not yet know what is meant by "burnt").

The estate of Joseph Loddle in 1754 included "3 Chiney Chocolate Cupps, one crackt — 3 shillings."

Jonathan Holmes of New York sold in 1751 "3 quart china japanned mugs."

William Beekman's inventory of 1795 included such china ware as "2 China Tureens 4 do. soup dishes" and "5 pcs ornamental China."

The *New York Commercial Advertiser* of April 13, 1811, lists for sale from the ship *America* from Canton:

"79 boxes each a dining set China, consisting of 121 to 205 pieces.

3 Elegant do. of 225 pieces"

The city directories of 1831 to 1835 list no less than fifty-four "China Stores" with addresses such as "Old Slip," 16, 129 and 164 The Bowery, "The corner of Pearl and Madison" and 289 Broadway.

Pride of personal possession played a very great part after 1785, and it is from this period that most of the exhibits come. Initials replaced armorials. Eagles chased away lions. The arms of New York found new forms on the China trade porcelain. As the nineteenth century wore on, the China trade found new forms and wares in China to delight the rapidly growing market of New York. It was the busiest market in America.

The careful records of such homes as Cherry Hill of the Van Rensselaers, Clermont of the Livingstons, Van Cortlandt Manor, and Sleepy Hollow have been supplemented by the painstaking work of the archeologists at Peebles Island whose contribution to this exhibition is among the most exciting and unexpected of its features.

The exhibition is arranged chronologically in four broad sections:

A. The Colonial Period, 1620–1780
B. The *Empress of China* and the First Five Years of the American Trade, 1785–1790
C. The First Century of the American China Trade, 1790–1880
D. The Last Hundred Years of the American China Trade, 1880–1984

There are no watertight divisions, although the greatest divide in style and taste is between the colonial period and the era of the *Empress of China*. While prominent buyers must have spanned both these periods, it was the changing pattern of trading which appears to have altered taste so radically between 1780 and 1790. This taste was no longer dictated by the needs of Europe. Indeed, the American influence can soon be seen on wares taken to the European market.

During 1784, thirty-four ships arrived at Canton, of which twenty-one were British (sailing both directly from England and from ports in India), four each were from France, Holland, and Denmark, and one was from America. Within fifteen years one-third of all the ships trading were American. This proportion remained until the close of the British East India Company monopoly in 1834 as the following table shows:

Ships Clearing the Port of Canton for Foreign Destinations

in	1784	1786	1790	1795	1800	1805	1810	1815	1820	1825	1830	1833
British	21	53	46	33	40	53	34	47	50	61	72	107
Dutch	4	5	3	—	—	—	—	2	—	—	5	8
French	4	1	2	—	—	—	—	—	—	—	5	7
Danish	4	3	1	—	4	2	—	—	—	—	1	4
Swedish	—	1	—	2	2	3	—	3	—	—	—	—
Spanish	—	3	1	2	—	—	—	—	—	—	—	—
Portuguese			(no records as they traded out of Macao)									
American	1	5	6	10	23	41	15	21	25	42	25	59
Prussian	—	—	—	—	—	—	—	—	—	—	—	1
Russian	—	—	—	—	—	2	—	—	—	—	—	—
Sardinian	—	—	—	—	—	—	—	—	—	—	1	—
Belgian	—	—	—	—	—	—	—	—	—	—	—	1
Hamburg	—	—	—	—	—	—	—	—	—	—	—	1
Mexican	—	—	—	—	—	—	—	—	—	—	—	1
	34	71	59	47	69	101	49	73	75	103	109	189

Source: Hosea Ballou Morse, *Chronicles of the East India Company Trading to China, 1635–1834.* 5 vols. Oxford, 1926–1929

The extent to which this trade was that of New York as opposed to that of other East Coast American ports needs further detailed investigation, but there is no doubt that by 1840 New York was the dominant port and by ten years later the only serious Atlantic port in the American China trade.

It is more difficult to be so precise with the objects which are the main focus of this exhibition. The aim has been to confine the exhibits solely to those which have New York provenance and usually New York ownership, although there have been one or two exceptions which are mentioned in the catalogue. The list of sailings would suggest that by 1840 a very high percentage of all American imports from China must have come to New York. New York certainly had a considerable share earlier, but most of the porcelain, lacquer, and other wares which survive in New York State have no certain provenance. Thus what *is* exhibited would pale into insignificance beside what *could* be exhibited were its history known.

But that is the challenge of history and the tantalizing imponderable of such a vast subject as New York and the China trade. Even now, this exhibition can do no more than introduce the subject—it is hoped in a way which will stimulate further inquiry.

In achieving this start some people outside The New-York Historical Society's own staff have contributed greatly to what has been achieved. Mrs. Charlotte Wilcoxen of Albany has been an historical inspiration for the earlier periods, as has Paul Huey, the senior archeologist at Peebles Island. Norman Rice of the Albany Institute provided much help and encouragement and Arlene Palmer Schwind, through her work on the Rhinelander papers, was able to provide exceptionally informative background material for those darker ages before 1785. Nothing would have appeared at all but for three months of typing from scribbled notes by

Angela and Genevieve in London. It is the bringing together of such diverse enthusiasms and goodwills which makes everything possible and worthwhile; even then it could hardly have happened without the persistent and efficient help of Elizabeth Currie, the Historical Society's Coordinator of Exhibitions, who has had to bear the burden of a far-flung supply line, and all encompassed by the relaxed atmosphere created by James Bell.

For me it has been a pleasure and privilege to have worked with such company.

David Sanctuary Howard
London. September 1983

The Colonial Period, 1620–1780

AI *The Colonial Period*

More than one and one-half centuries elapsed between the arrival of the first Chinese porcelain in America and the voyage of the *Empress of China* in 1784. Very few whole pieces from the seventeenth century have survived, but excavations in New York City and along the Hudson River have provided evidence that such wares were traded on a substantial scale.

Seventeenth-century New Yorkers did not ordinarily buy porcelain of the finest grade, but in the eighteenth century such wealthy colonial families as the Livingstons purchased porcelain of a quality which would have graced the grandest English drawing room. The style of the porcelain was no different from that sold in Europe; indeed the only sudden change in taste arose after the American Revolution, when independence produced new trading patterns.

The story of New York and its trade with China begins with the porcelain with which the Dutch East India Company filled its warehouses in Holland. From Holland, Dutch residents and merchants imported the ware to New Amsterdam.

The correspondence of one family, the Van Rensselaers, reveals how it acquired at least some of its Chinese porcelain. Susanna Van Rensselaer wrote from Amsterdam on April 9, 1662, to her brother, Jeremias, at Fort Orange (Albany):

I have already transacted some business for you in buying your household goods. I had much trouble in procuring the small table plates as not so many are being made, for the people now all use pewter, so that I couldn't get any better ones.

Two decades later in 1684 it was Catrina Darvall of New York, a sister of Jeremias's wife, Maria, who was supplying the Van Rensselaers with their Chinese porcelain:

. . . I am also sending two large porcelain jars costing the sum of fl. 5:10 for which you must send the money to your daughter Maria to buy a cape for her. Please do not forget to send down the peas. I shall send the bags by the next sloop.

Some seventy objects illustrate the colonial period in this exhibition. Most are shards. Many whole pieces have probably survived from colonial New York in addition to those included here, but only those with certain provenances are exhibited.

References: A. J. F. van Laer, trans. and ed., *Correspondence of Jeremias van Rensselaer, 1651–1672* (Albany: State University of New York, 1932); A. J. F. van Laer, trans. and ed., *Correspondence of Maria van Rensselaer, 1669–1689* (Albany: State University of New York, 1935).

Research: Mrs. Charlotte Wilcoxen, Albany Institute of History and Art

A2 *Two Blue and White Bowls*, c. 1630–1670
Diameter: 4½ inches
Loan: Sleepy Hollow Restorations, Tarrytown, New York

These bowls, which are decorated in an underglaze blue with a kylin and an artemis leaf, are unmistakably Ming in style. They could have been made at any time after the first quarter of the seventeenth century. Their general form and painting suggest that they may have been made in approximately 1630, while the leaf on the base argues for a later date, perhaps 1670.

The bowls were found between 1940 and 1945 in the general area of the wharf along the Hudson River at Philipse Manor, which was north of Getty Square in Yonkers. Unfortunately, details of their discovery are imprecise. The bowls may have fallen from the wharf before 1674, when "Yonker" or "Gentleman" Van der Donck owned the property, or about 1681, when Frederick Philipse, a Dutch carpenter and successful entrepreneur who purchased the land from Van der Donck, was equipping his first house. Unless an exact location can be established, the date of the bowls remains between 1630 and 1670 and the term "Transitional" best describes them. Certainly, the bowls are the two earliest, almost whole pieces of Chinese porcelain with a proven New York history.

A2

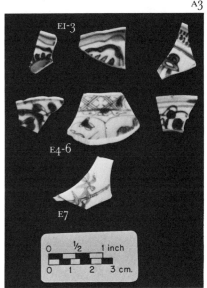

A3

A3 *Excavations at Schuyler Flats*
Loan: New York State, Office of Parks, Recreation, and Historic Preservation, Bureau of Historic Sites. Archaeological artifacts excavated at Schuyler Flats, Saratoga-Capital State Park Region

Philip Pieterson Schuyler arrived in New Netherland about 1650. In 1672 from the Van Rensselaers he purchased a large farm immediately north of Albany on the Hudson River. The farmhouse burned in 1759, but the Schuyler family rebuilt it and occupied it until 1910. The building stood until 1962, when it burned again.

The Van Rensselaers had established the original farm in the 1640s. On level ground close to the river, it had been an Indian trading post in earlier times. The farm passed to Pieter Schuyler, whose brother-in-law was Robert Livingston. Pieter Schuyler became mayor of Albany in 1680. He was a powerful influence in Indian politics, and accompanied four native chiefs to London in 1710. With Sir William Johnson, he was the leading English figure in Indian affairs in eighteenth-century New York.

The Heldeberg Workshop of the New York State Department of Parks and Recreation oversaw the excavation of the site between 1971 and 1974. As expected, Schuyler Flats proved a rich resource. Not only had the farm been occupied continuously since 1640, but as a trading post it had been fortified. It had also served as a military campground during the Indian wars of the early eighteenth century, the Seven Years War, and the American Revolution. The original cellar yielded many finds from the first half of the seventeenth century, including Dutch Delft tiles, clay pipes, trading knives, gun parts, beads, and many types of ceramics. The cellar eventually collapsed and was filled in sometime after 1730.

E 1–3. Three fragments, probably from two different small, blue and white Wan Li (Ming) bowls, c. 1620. (ASF. 1971.37/80/127)

E 4–6. Three fragments from different blue and white pieces of Kang Hsi porcelain, two bowls and a molded saucer, c. 1700–1720. (ASF. 1971.41; ASF. 1971.43; and ASF. 1972.1221)

E 7. A fragment from a small, blue and white, Yung Cheng plate or saucer, c. 1730. (ASF. 1971.25)

A4 *Excavations at Johnson Hall*
Loan: New York State, Office of Parks, Recreation, and Historic Preservation, Bureau of Historic Sites. Archaeological artifacts excavated at Johnson Hall State Historic Site, Saratoga-Capital State Park Region

Sir William Johnson was born in Ireland in 1715. At the age of twenty-two or twenty-three he came to New York to manage an estate in the Mohawk Valley belonging to his uncle, Vice Admiral Sir Peter Warren. In 1745, when war broke out on New York's frontier, Johnson negotiated with the Indians of the Six Nations and ensured their neutrality. Active in the colony's militia, he had risen to the rank of major general by 1755, when with the help of the Mohawks he defeated the French at the Battle of Lake George. That year he was created a baronet; the following year he became superintendent of Indian affairs north of the Ohio River. In 1763 he began building Johnson Hall, fourteen miles north of the Mohawk River. Johnson Hall was a thriving estate at the time of his sudden death in 1774. Johnson's son, John, succeeded to the baronetcy, but the estate was confiscated in 1779 after he opposed the American Revolution and raised a loyalist regiment in Canada. After the war the estate was sold; it remained in private hands until 1906.

During the 1950s and again in the late 1970s archaeologists attempted to discover the exact positions of the various houses at Johnson Hall and the location of a tunnel linking the main hall with an outhouse.

Archaeologists also searched for a stockade line, built in 1763. Many of these excavations proved inconclusive, but they produced large quantities of ceramic shards, particularly of saltglazed stoneware dating from the 1750s and creamware and pearlware from the 1760s. These, together with some Delft, comprise more than ninety-five percent of the shards found; the remainder, a total of sixteen shards, is Chinese porcelain.

In view of their small number, the pieces of Chinese porcelain may have been special or decorative items, perhaps presents or occasional purchases. They may have been purchased in Albany or New York, or even brought from Europe. The creamware formed services, for Sir William's agent in New York wrote on September 5, 1769:

. . . the Table Crockery I now send are quite new fashioned, several principal Families have lately got them over from England, they are very much Admired, but come Very high — tho' those I now Send you are at least 25 p Cent Cheaper

A4

A4

A5

than any I have Seen; I hope you will approve of my Sending them rather than the Common White Ones (of which indeed do not believe I could have picked up your Quantity in Town) for I do not See why you Should not be in the Fashion as well as anybody Else.

There is no evidence of the date of the deposits, but it could be anytime between 1765 and the Civil War. Most of the ceramics came from a large storage pit in the center of a building identified in 1774 in Sir William's probate inventory as the "Indian Store." The Chinese porcelain dates between approximately 1620 and the end of the eighteenth century, and includes one or two rare fragments.

D 1. A blue and white fragment from a small Wan Li (Ming) or Transitional dish, c. 1620–30. (AJH 1950s 463 57)

D 2. Part of a small, late, blue and white

Wan Li or Transitional bowl similar to ones being traded by the Dutch, c. 1610–20. (AJH 1950s 463 24)

D 3. An unusual piece of Chinese soft paste porcelain with blue and white decoration. It dates from the late seventeenth century. (AJH 1981 295)

D 4. Fragment of a small bowl with blue and white decoration. It is similar to a tea-bowl fragment found in Jamestown, Virginia, with a cyclical date of 1666. (AJH 1950s 463 5)

D 5. An almost complete underglaze blue saucer, c. 1735–45. (AJH 1950s 468 5)

D 6. A fragment of a plate finely decorated *en grisaille* with flowers, c. 1755. This may have been in part polychrome and the enamels may have disappeared. (AJH 1958 466 61)

A5 *Arita Shaving Bowl,* c. 1680–1700, Japanese

Diameter: 10¾ inches
Loan: Sleepy Hollow Restorations, Tarrytown, New York (V.C. 64.102)

This shaving bowl is decorated in an underglaze blue, with a pinkish, red thin wash and gilding. The neck piece is cut away, with two holes on the opposite rim for a ribbon. The bowl could thus be tied around the neck and rest on the chest when in use.

It was no accident that late seventeenth-century shaving bowls should have been made in Japan. The wars which attended the fall of the Ming dynasty reduced the flow of Chinese porcelain to a low ebb between 1640 and the early 1680s. Throughout this period, Japanese porcelain followed the same trade routes to America via Batavia and Europe that Chinese exports took. Chinese porcelain makers had reasserted their dominance over the market by the early eighteenth century, two decades after the kilns at Ching-te Chen reopened.

In 1884, William Caldwell gave this bowl to his niece, Catherine Elizabeth Beck Van Cortlandt (1818–1895). He told her that a Captain Long of Newport, Rhode Island, had originally imported it. Although the Van Cortlandt family had owned the bowl for a century, they sold it at auction in 1941. It was later returned to Van Cortlandt Manor.

A6 *Blanc de Chine Figure Group*, c. 1700

Height: 8⅜ inches
Loan: Sleepy Hollow Restorations, Tarrytown, New York (v.c. 72.1)

This group is one of the more ambitious creations of Fukien Province, where porcelain makers produced such figures from the end of the Ming dynasty, c. 1640, at Tehua, upriver from Foochow. Similar pieces have many minor variations. The potter might face the figures toward each other or outward. The groups were caricatures of the merchants and their antics as the Chinese saw them. The European figures were not based on a specific model, or at least one that has been identified.

This piece came to Van Cortlandt Manor as a gift from Miss Charlotte Van Cortlandt, but has a history in the family from colonial times. Whole groups of this type with American provenance are very rare but not unknown, as witness the *blanc de chine* shard of the same date at Clermont (cat. A11).

A7 *Teapot*, c. 1700–1720

Length: 6 inches (over handle)
Loan: National Society of Colonial Dames, Van Cortlandt Mansion

This small, bullet-shaped teapot with molded panels is decorated in the *famille verte* style with enameling added in Europe, almost certainly in Holland. Although the teapot has a long history in the Van Cortlandt family, there is no record of whether they owned it in colonial times. Its decoration is entirely consistent with pieces of the period sold in America.

A8 *Small Armorial Bowl*, c. 1716

Diameter: 7¾ inches
Loan: Mottahedeh Collection

This bowl belongs to a dinner service made in China in the Japanese Imari style about 1716. The service is most unusual in its repetition of the arms five times on each larger piece. Only one other known service was painted this way.

The arms are of the Horsemonden fam-

A6

A7

A8

ily. Daniel Horsemonden, who was born in 1691 and died in Flatbush in 1778, almost certainly ordered the service. A cousin, John Horsemonden, who was a supercargo and a member of the East India Company's Council at Canton in 1721, probably brought him the service. A number of members of the family came to the colonies in the seventeenth and eighteenth centuries. Colonel Warham Horsemonden emigrated in the middle of the seventeenth century to Virginia, where he became a member of the colony's governing council. He returned to England at the restoration of Charles II to the throne in 1660, leaving his friend John Washington, a direct ancestor of the first president of the United States.

A9 *Excavations at Hanover Square, New York City*

Early records indicate that Hanover Square in lower Manhattan served as a public common as early as 1637, when "elegant residences...very close to the river" surrounded it. Close to Wall Street, the square is situated where Hanover, Pearl, Stone, and William Streets meet Old Slip. Nearby, 119 Pearl Street was the home of Captain Kidd, who was charged with piracy and executed in England in 1699. New York's first newspaper, the *New York Gazette*, was printed at 3 Pearl Street in 1726. John Broome (cat. c59), an important China trade merchant, lived over his tea store in Hanover Square. It was one of the few public places not to have its name changed after the Revolution. A great fire destroyed it in 1835.

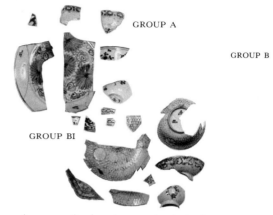

A9

GROUP A

GROUP BI

An excavation by a team under the leadership of Dr. Nan Rothschild of Barnard College has revealed a broad range of porcelain at the Hanover Square site, from Transitional fragments, c. 1630, to pieces from the early nineteenth century, and including items from the stock of a Chinaware shop, c. 1790.

For the purposes of this exhibition, porcelain from Hanover Square has been divided into the following categories:

GROUP A Blue and White Late Ming/Transitional to Kang Hsi Pieces, 1630–1720
GROUP B i. Fine Quality Pieces, 1720–1765
ii. Special Order Pieces, 1785–1795
GROUP C Mid to Late Eighteenth-Century Blue and White Pieces, 1745–1800
GROUP D Cups and Mugs, 1785–1810
GROUP E China Shop Ware, 1790–1800

* * *

GROUP A Blue and White Late Ming/Transitional to Kang Hsi Pieces, 1630–1720
A1. Small fragments of late Ming/Transitional ware. (624/39.282)
A2. Two fragments of a provincial bowl from the late seventeenth or early eighteenth century. This ware was very common in Southeast Asia and was traded by the Dutch in Europe. (624/39.108)
A3. Large fragments of a late seventeenth- or early eighteenth-century provincial por-

celain saucer dish. (624/293.32)
A4. and A5. Two fragments of Kang Hsi teabowls, c. 1720. (624/47.63 and 624/808.13)

GROUP B i. Fine Quality Pieces, 1720–1765
B1. Small fragment of a good quality cup, Kang Hsi, c. 1700. (624/118.43)
B2. Rim fragment from a plate of fine quality, blue and white with *rouge de fer* and gold border, c. 1730. (624/149.3)
B3. Two very fine quality rim fragments with *rouge de fer*, gold diaper, and blue enamel, c. 1730–1735. (624/1196.2 and 624/1196.3)
B4. Large rim fragment of lobed octagonal teapot stand, with diapers and central scene with figures, c. 1760. (624/256.14)
B5. Two fragments from a saucer dish with petal design in pale red. (624/293.88 and 624/293.91)
B6. Three fragments of a covered sugar bowl with panels and pink trellis, c. 1770. (624/96.26; 624/96.18/19; 624/96.29)

GROUP B ii. Special Order Pieces, 1785–1795
B7. Two rim fragments with diaper border and butterfly, exactly as used for the Cincinnati service (cat. B3), c. 1785. (624/256.138 and 624/256.176)
B8. Large part of a leaf-shaped sauce boat stand, possibly originally with initial or gilt flower spray in the center, c. 1790. (624/279.507)
B9. Large fragment of a saucer dish, with an underglaze blue diaper border, central shield for initials, and mantling, c. 1790. (624/279.500–503)

GROUP C Middle to Late Eighteenth-Century Blue and White, 1745–1800
C1. Fine fragment of plate with boy riding a buffalo, c. 1745. (624/771.6)
C2. Nearly complete plate of inexpensive blue underglaze, c. 1745. (624/279.394; 624/279.396; *et seq.*)

C3. Rim section of shaped tray or dish, c. 1765. (624/261.169)
C4. Substantial fragments of dish with tree, flower, and birds in center, c. 1765. (624/293.9; 624/293.16; 624/293.30)
C5. Two large fragments of milk jug with flowers and classical figuration, c. 1765. (624/96.54 and 624/147.34)
C6. Large fragment of jug with terrace scene, c. 1755. (624/256.130)
C7. Fragment of saucer with simulated cut-away border and central lake scene, c. 1800 or later. (624/139.143)

GROUP D Late Eighteenth- to Early Nineteenth-Century Cups and Mugs, 1785–1810
D1. Large part of underglaze blue cylindrical mug with trellis border, c. 1790. (624/256.127 *et seq.*)
D2. Underglaze blue mug with simple handle, rough trellis-like floral scroll border, and a river scene, c. 1810 or later. (624/249.26 and 624/261.24, *et seq.*)

A9

GROUP D

D3. Substantial part of large teabowl of period and style similar to D2. (624/279.261, 624/279.273, and others)
D4. Section of underglaze blue floral cup with passion flower, c. 1800 or later. (624/118.8–11)
D5. Teabowl with polychrome floral decoration, c. 1785. (624/147.41)

GROUP E China Shop Ware, c. 1790–1800
E1. and E2. Two of a very large number of shards of a tea service with scattered floral border and a wavy dotted line sur-

GROUP C

GROUP B2

A9

GROUP E

A9

A10

rounding flowers, c. 1790. (624/1196.1 and 624/1196.4)

E3. Good quality fine porcelain shard from teabowl with gilt trellis design, c. 1788. (624/783.1)

E4. Saucer fragment with blue enamel border, c. 1800. (624/1196.5)

Excavation of the Seven Hanover Square block in 1981 was sponsored by the New York City Landmarks Preservation Commission, and supported by the developer of the site, Swig, Weiler, and Arnow. The investigations were carried out by a team of archaeologists under the direction of Arnold Pickman and Diana Rockman of New York University and Nan Rothschild

of Barnard College, Columbia University. Ceramic analysis was done by Meta Janowitz of the City University Graduate Center, with Kate Morgan of the Graduate Center and Nancy Stehling as laboratory directors.

A10 *Teapot*, c. 1735
Height: 4½ inches
Loan: Sleepy Hollow Restorations, Tarrytown, New York (V.C. 58.185)

This teapot, from the Van Cortlandt family, has brushwork typical of the first quarter of the eighteenth century. The underglaze blue painting of flowers and leaves is characteristic of the period. A band of

scrollwork is at the mouth and on the cover. While the decoration is modest, the porcelain is of good quality.

Reference: Joseph T. Butler, *Sleepy Hollow Restorations: A Cross Section of the Collections* (Tarrytown: Sleepy Hollow Restorations Collection, 1983), 94.

A11 *Excavations at Clermont*
Loan: New York State, Office of Parks, Recreation, and Historic Preservation, Bureau of Historic Sites, Clermont State Historic Site, Taconic State Park Region

Considerable archaeological work took place between 1974 and 1980 on a site between the house at Clermont and the Hudson River. The house was rebuilt after British naval and land forces burned it on their advance up the Hudson in 1777.

Most of the ruins of the first house, built by Robert Livingston in 1728, were on hard ground which also supported a driveway to the west of the house. It was here that excavators found a great many Livingston family artifacts, including iron- and brassware, English creamware, and a considerable quantity of Chinese porcelain. From many pieces the glaze had burned off, indicating a temperature of at least 1,000° C at the time of destruction. The oriental porcelain falls into three groups:

GROUP A   Pieces which the Livingstons inherited by marriage, for they were related to the great Dutch families of the Hudson Valley, or brought with them. (See "Excavations at Schuyler Flats.")

GROUP B   Pieces probably purchased when the house was built

GROUP C   Porcelain bought between 1728 and 1777

The size of the services that Robert Livingston bought is not clear. He may only have bought sets of two or three dozen plates, or small coffee sets, instead of the huge services of from 400 to 800 pieces sometimes commissioned for European houses. The quality was of the very best and would have graced any English country house. This can be judged from the shards illustrated, some of which represent much larger numbers of each pattern. The selection illustrated gives an idea of the range of porcelain in one wealthy household in the mid-eighteenth century.

GROUP A   Pieces probably inherited

A1. Part of a Kang Hsi bowl with finely painted Chinese mark, underglaze blue, c. 1700. (ACL 1980 1111)

A2. Fragment of a chocolate cup or small mug, blue and white, c. 1710. (ACL 1975 134)

A3. Fragment of plate, underglaze blue, c. 1720. (ACL 1975 140)

A4. Two fragments of the base of a Kang Hsi blue and white, hexagonal saltcellar, c. 1710. (ACL 1975 144 and ACL 1975 145)

A5. Fragment of the base of a *blanc de chine* figure with two feet attached, c. 1700. (ACL 1979 917)

A6. Fragments of the rim of a *famille verte* punch bowl, c. 1720. (ACL 1980 1113)

GROUP B   Pieces probably purchased when the house was built

B1. Fragments of a dinner service plate with aquatic plants and ducks in the center and similar decoration on the rim, c. 1730–1735. (ACL 1975 134)

B2. Three fragments of a very fine *famille rose* coffee cup, c. 1730. Heat and chemical effects have turned the enamels grey. (ACL 1978 807)

B3. Fragment of the rim of a blue and white plate with trellis and flowered rockwork, c. 1735. (ACL 1980 149)

B4. Large fragment of a plate with blue and white floral and trellis decoration on the rim and an "an hua" or "secret" central design, c. 1730. (ACL 1975 146)

GROUP C   Porcelain bought between 1728 and 1777

C1. Fragments of a Chinese Imari circular dish of about fourteen inches, c. 1740. (ACL 1976 265)

C2. Piece of blue and white dinner service, 1740. (ACL 1980 1111)

C3. Two fragments of a Chinese plate with river scene and bridge,

AII GROUP B

c. 1770. (ACL 1975 134)

C4. Base of a teabowl with underglaze blue and polychrome enamel. The enamel has been burned off or altered in color by burning, c. 1760. (ACL 1975 134)

C5. Fragments of the rim of a teabowl with trellis and floral festoon border, c. 1775. (ACL 1975 134)

C6. A number of fragments from a milk jug, and probably also a teapot, in orange, sepia, and *famille rose*, c. 1760. (ACL 1975 134)

A12 *Armorial Mug*, c. 1750
Height: 5 inches
Loan: Mr. and Mrs. Charles A. Atkins

This mug with plain handle is of a standard design for armorial services made in China for the British market. The rim has chain decoration, the sides have floral sprays, and the arms are of Roddam of Northumberland impaling Clinton.

Robert Roddam, a naval captain stationed at New York, married a niece of Governor George Clinton on April 24, 1749. Mrs. Roddam died in childbirth in Decem-

AII GROUP A

AII GROUP C

A12

ber 1750. Captain Roddam, who was a prisoner of the French during the Seven Years War, and later rose to the rank of Admiral of the Red, died in 1808 at age eighty-eight. Although he married twice more, he had no children.

The service of which this mug forms a part must have been ordered in 1749 or 1750. The sad story of the first Mrs. Roddam enables a very exact dating. Captain Roddam's brother, Collingwood, who was in the East India Company maritime service, probably brought the porcelain from China.

A13 *Punch Bowl*, c. 1760
Diameter: 15¾ inches
Collection of The New-York Historical Society, gift of Gouverneur Kemble (1921.13)

This rich *famille rose* punch bowl, painted in overlapping lotus leaves in variegated pink, and with panels of gilding, was popular in the English market, c. 1755–1765. A

A13

considerable number of pieces of this decoration were also in the cargo of the Spanish galleon which Captain Hyde Parker captured in 1763.

The bowl belonged to Isaac Gouverneur (1749–1800), a New York City merchant. Gouverneur's nephew, Gouverneur Kemble (1786–1875), inherited it, and the family used it at "Cockloft Hall," its mansion in Newark on the Passaic River. Among those often present were Washington Irving, Henry Brevoort, James K. Paulding, and Henry Ogden.

Reference: *New-York Historical Society Quarterly* 5 (1921), 78.

A14 *Oval Platter*, c. 1760
Length: 13½ inches
Loan: Collection of Historic Cherry Hill, Albany, New York (134)

As far as is known, this shaped platter has a unique design: houses on a peninsula in

A14

the foreground and buildings on a second peninsula in the middle distance, all within a spearhead border, and European scrollwork on the rim. The platter is the only known piece of its service. It has been in the Van Rensselaer house at Cherry Hill since colonial times and could be from the first dinner service that the family used there after the construction of the house in 1768.

The service probably acted as the pattern for the DeWitt Clinton service (cat. c66), for Stephen Van Rensselaer and DeWitt Clinton were colleagues, spending much time planning the Erie Canal, and both services are apparently unique. Even the number of rocks in the foreground is the same, and the outward facing spearhead of this pattern on both is unusual.

A15 *Punch Bowl*, c. 1765
Diameter: 21½ inches
Loan: Albany Institute of History and Art (U 1972.25.1)

This massive and heavily potted bowl is of a type and decoration popular in Europe in the 1760s. With floral decoration in *famille rose*, it must have been specially ordered in China, possibly through a merchant in New York.

Mr. and Mrs. John V. L. Pruyn of Albany formerly owned the bowl. It was at one time known as the "Regents Punchbowl," since Mr. Pruyn often used it to serve punch to the Board of Regents of New York when he was chancellor. There is a legend that the bowl once belonged to Governor Daniel Tompkins (1774–1825) of New York, but if so, it must also have had an earlier owner, since

A15   A16 DISH

it was made at about the same time as the governor's birth. The Pruyn family of Albany, prominent in the business and social life of the city in the nineteenth and twentieth centuries, was descended from Frans Jansz Pruyn, a tailor, who was living in Albany as early as 1661. It appears that he was of Flemish rather than Dutch ancestry. Although he seems to have been a substantial citizen of Albany, in 1699 he was refused the right to take the oath of allegiance because he was considered a Papist.

A16 *Centerpiece Dish and Plates*, c. 1765
Diameter: 9½ inches
Loans: Centerpiece dish and plate (illustrated), Mr. and Mrs. Samuel Schwartz; plate, The Metropolitan Museum of Art, gift of James Delancey Verplanck and John Bayard Rodgers Verplanck, 1939 (39.184.29)

The shape and decoration of this dish are derived from Meissen porcelain. The dish was used as a tray to hold a porcelain fruit basket and various condiment vessels. The floral decoration is entirely European in style, and was most popular in German and Scandinavian countries. The dish and plate were formerly owned by Samuel and Judith (Crommelin) Verplanck, who lived at 3 Wall Street from 1763 to 1803.

A16 PLATE

AI7

AI7 *Plate*, c. 1770
Diameter: 8¾ inches
Loan: Mr. and Mrs. Samuel Schwartz

This octagonal dinner plate is painted in the center with flowers growing out of rockwork and with a pink diaper well. Sprays of flowers within a spearhead rim decorate the border. The design was popular on both sides of the Atlantic. Samuel and Judith (Crommelin) Verplanck formerly owned the plate (see cat. AI6).

AI8 *Small Part Service*, c. 1770
Loan: The National Society of Colonial Dames, Van Cortlandt Mansion

The service is decorated in underglaze blue and *famille rose* enamels. With figures in the center and elaborately patterned rims, it is typical of services of its period. The service has probably been at Van Cortlandt Mansion, now in Van Cortlandt Park on Broadway and 242nd Street, since colonial times. Frederick Van Cortlandt built the house in 1748. The service has probably been there from the mansion's second decade. Great figures frequented the house and may have used the service. In 1781 alone, visitors included George Washington, Rochambeau, and the Duke of Clarence, later William IV of England.

AI8

AI9

AI9 *Excavations at Crown Point Barracks*
Loan: New York State, Office of Parks, Restoration, and Historic Preservation, Bureau of Historic Sites. Crown Point State Historic Site, Saratoga-Capital State Park Region

The excavations of the Crown Point Barracks on Lake Champlain have revealed a collection of small porcelain shards from before 1773. The barracks were occupied by British troops between 1759 and 1773. The officers' and soldiers' quarters were quite separate. In spite of the relaxing of discipline at isolated frontier posts of this sort, it is surprising that all the shards of Chinese porcelain were found at the quarters of the enlisted men, since the officers' quarters also had adequate waste pits. Whether the officers and men dined in the same quarters, or whether shards from the officers' quarters were thrown down the wastepits at the soldiers' quarters, or whether the soldiers dined from various odd pieces of Chinese porcelain while the officers used plate is not clear.

A20 *Soup Plate and Dinner Plate*, c. 1775
Diameter: 9¼ inches
Loan: Anonymous

This service with green sawtooth enamel and flower sprays on bamboo was typical of its time. Its history, however, was exceptional.

The arms are painted as Alexander, Earl of Stirling, quartering MacDonald. The arms are correct except for the use of a beaver crest instead of a bear. Alexander was the last recognized Earl of Stirling. He died in 1739 without any known heir. The original grant of Earl of Stirling and Viscount Canada was so sweeping, though, that any heir, however distant, could possibly be included.

In 1757 William Alexander, son of William Alexander who had been surveyor general of New Jersey in 1714 and a member of the Councils of New Jersey and New York, went to England and claimed the title. The House of Lords would not recognize his right, though, until he had "made

A20

out his claim." Undeterred, William Alexander styled himself Lord Stirling until his death in 1783.

Sometime after 1770, Lord Stirling must have ordered a Chinese armorial service. When it arrived in London on its way to New York, however, the War of Independence had commenced and all trade had ceased. It is almost certain that he never saw the service. It must have been sold off in England, for pieces have since turned up there, so far all in unused condition.

The British captured Lord Stirling at the Battle of Long Island and acknowledged his title in their dispatches. They later ex-

changed him and he was on active duty when he died in January 1783. Two daughters survived him, "Lady Mary," who married Robert Watts, and "Lady Kitty," who married Colonel William Duer.

A21 *Small Part Service*, c. 1775
Loan: New York State, Office of Parks, Recreation, and Historic Preservation, Bureau of Historic Sites. John Jay Homestead State Historic Sites, Taconic State Park Region

These pieces, a tureen stand, small platter, and gravy boat and stand, are from a serv-

ice made about 1775. The design shows floral sprays and a dogtooth and chain border. The initials "J.J." are in the center. There seems to be little doubt from the style of the porcelain that this service was ordered before the war, and may even have been delivered before the commencement of hostilities. The initials belong to John Jay, who was secretary in 1773 of the Royal Commission which settled the boundary dispute between New York and New Jersey. By 1779 he was chief justice of New York; from 1784 to 1790 he was first secretary of foreign affairs. (See cat. c52, where a punch bowl is illustrated.)

A21

The *Empress of China* and the First Five Years of the American Trade, 1785–1790

BI OUTSIDE

BI *Punch Bowl*, 1784–1785
Diameter: 15½ inches
Loan: New Jersey State Museum Collection, Trenton, gift of Richard V. Lindabury (69.244 A-C)

This bowl is decorated on the outside with a gilt and red Greek key pattern, floral swags, and tassels, and with a spray of flowers on either side. On the inside it has pink scale diaper at the rim surrounding a well-painted, three-masted merchant vessel. The ship is flying an early American flag with a ribbon reading "John Green — Empress of China — Commander." The bowl is important both stylistically and as an historical document.

The *Empress of China* sailed from New York on February 22, 1784. Robert Morris of Philadelphia and Daniel Parker & Co. of New York outfitted her at a cost of $120,000. Her captain was John Green; Samuel Shaw, who had served until recently as aide-de-camp to General Henry Knox, was the investors' "supercargo" or agent. The vessel returned from Canton less than fifteen months later with a cargo which included silk, teas, porcelain, fans, satin breeches, window blinds, and umbrellas.

As far as is known, this is the only piece of porcelain that can be traced to the *Empress of China*'s return voyage. The bowl has a turned mahogany stand which has been considerably damaged over the years. The interior is painted exactly like a similar bowl for the ship *Grand Turk*, except that the name differs and a second scroll on the *Grand Turk* bowl reads "At Canton 1786." Every detail of the hull and rigging matches, including the flag. This similarity throws doubt on the accuracy of the painting.

Reference: For an illustration of the *Grand Turk* bowl, see Jean McClure Mudge, *Chinese Export Porcelain for the American Trade, 1785–1835* (Newark: University of Delaware Press, 1962), 108.

BI INSIDE

BIA *Painting of Samuel Shaw*, early twentieth century
Dimensions: 37 inches by 30 inches
Medium: Oil on canvas
Loan: Robert B. Minturn

Samuel Shaw was the chief architect of a taste for Chinese export porcelain which has become the most lasting evidence of the American China trade. Shaw was born in Boston in 1754 and died in 1794. He served as General George Washington's aide-de-camp during the Revolutionary War, and was also on the staff of General Henry Knox. He was the senior "super-cargo," or investors' agent, on the *Empress of China* during the first American voyage to Canton, 1784–1785. He later served as the first United States consul in Canton. John Johnston (1752–1813) painted Shaw's portrait; appropriately, the *Empress of China* rests at anchor on the horizon. This is a good copy of the original, painted by H. R. Burdick in the early twentieth century.

B2 *Advertisement*, August 12, 1785
Collection of The New-York Historical Society

Although Major Samuel Shaw sailed as supercargo on the *Empress of China* in February 1784 and returned on that ship the

following spring, he ordered more porcelain in Canton than was ready for the return journey.

In particular, the porcelain with the underglaze blue border popular on European services and the emblem of the Society of the Cincinnati followed on the ship *Pallas*. This lists over 120 "chests" and some "tubs" of "china."

On August 12 in the *Baltimore Advertiser* appeared an advertisement which read in part:

"Table sets of the best Nankin blue and white stone china.... Ditto with the arms of the Order of Cincinnati; Bowls — best blue and white Stone China in sets; blue and white Stone China Pint Sneakers; Mugs — best Stone China in Sets; Small Tureens with Covers; Wash-hand Guglets and Basins."

B3 *Plate*, 1785
Diameter: 9⅞ inches
Loan: Mrs. Mildred Mottahedeh

With a shaped wavy edge, this plate has a complicated underglaze blue rim design which had been used on armorial porcelain for the British market for at least five years. At the center, in her left hand, the Angel of Fame holds the ribbon and badge of the Society of the Cincinnati, painted in enamels and gilding.

Despite the mention in the *Baltimore Advertiser* (cat. B2), there was no great rush to buy this unusual ware, perhaps because it was appropriate only to the small and select group of men who comprised the membership of the Society. George Washington,

B3

for one, did not avail himself of the opportunity to buy any until nearly a year later, when he bought most or all of the 306 remaining pieces.

The only surviving records of purchase indicate the sale of pieces to Washington and to Colonel Henry Lee, the father of General Robert E. Lee. Through the marriage of Martha Washington's great granddaughter to Robert E. Lee, the pieces of the services were probably mixed. Henry du Pont later acquired about half the known pieces, some seventy, including about a dozen shapes from soup tureen to custard cup. In a recent article on Society of the Cincinnati porcelain, Dr. Quentin Feller noted 129 pieces in both public and private collections.

References: John Quentin Feller, "China Trade Porcelain Decorated with the Emblem of the Society of the Cincinnati," *The Magazine ANTIQUES*, 118, no. 4 (Oct. 1980), 460–468. Susan Gray Detweiler, *George Washington's Chinaware* (New York: Harry N. Abrams, Inc., 1982), 208–211.

B4

B4 *Small Punch Bowl*, c. 1787
Diameter: 7¹¹⁄₁₆ inches
Collection of The New-York Historical Society, gift of Mrs. Fanny F. Clark (1923.27)

Decorated in the same style as the preceeding entry, and similar to the Cincinnati service for General Washington, this bowl has an armorial in addition to the initials "G.S.D." The armorial is quarterly first and fourth: "a cross bow between two bolts"; second: "a green garb (wheat sheaf) on a hillock"; third: "azure a fess indented between three bezants (gold roundels)." It is assumed to be the armorial of Gerardus

Duyckinck (1723–1797), although this is not recorded in standard European armorial works (see cat. B6).

B5

B5 *Teabowls and Saucers*, c. 1787–1790
Diameter of saucer: 6¼ inches
Loan: The Newark Museum, bequest of Marcus L. Ward (21.381.A–G)

This partial tea service, with an underglaze blue border decoration very similar to General Washington's Cincinnati porcelain (cat. B3), has the initials "C.V.D." on a shield within a floral mantling. The initials belong to Catherine Vanderpool Van Dyke (1741–1823) of Newark, New Jersey, who married the Newark merchant James Van Dyke (1740–1828) on June 5, 1765. The will of James Van Dyke, dated 1823 and probated 1828, included "1 Blue sett tea China, one set pencil'd do. $4.00." The service entered the United States via the port of New York.

Reference: "2,000 Years of Chinese Ceramics," *Newark Museum Quarterly* (Summer/ Fall 1977), 71 ff.

B6

B6 *Teabowl and Tray*, c. 1787
Height of bowl: 2 inches
Collection of The New-York Historical Society, gift of Mrs. Fanny F. Clark (1923.23 and 1923.30)

Decorated with a detailed underglaze blue border of butterflies and diaper, as on General Washington's Cincinnati service,

this porcelain has a shield with a floral surrounding and the initials "A.D." The bowl and tray are part of a tea service of which a number of bowls and plates still exist. The initials belonged to Ann Duyckinck. In 1752, Ann Rapelje (1733–1789) married Gerardus Duyckinck. Although family tradition has considered this their wedding porcelain, it was probably made about thirty-five years later and purchased when such porcelain became available on the American market.

B7 *Voyage of the Albany Sloop* Experiment, 1785–1787

In the whole history of the American China trade there was no more stirring episode than the voyage between 1785 and 1787 of the tiny Albany sloop *Experiment*. A tantalizing question mark still hangs over the identification of surviving pieces from the cargo. Certainly the tea has long been drunk and the "costly damask silk" faded and torn, but there still must be examples of "the thirteen sets of China ware to order." The only recorded family names thought to be connected with the cargo are Johnson, Ten Eyck, and Livingston. Possible examples are given below.

The extract below, from *The Annals of Albany* by Joel Munsell, provides the outline of the story:

In the fall of 1785, the sloop Experiment, *80 tons burden, Capt. Stewart Dean, was fitted out at this port for China. It was very properly considered a hazardous voyage for so small a craft. She was laden with assorted cargo, for a regular trading expedition, and was the second adventure from the United States to Canton. She left New York on the 18th December, and was absent eighteen months. Her return trip was made in four months and twelve days, with a cargo consisting principally of teas and nankins. Several pieces of costly damask silk were also brought to order, or for family gifts. One of the heir-looms in the family of a descendant of the mate of the* Experiment, *residing in Schenectady, is a dress, made of the silk referred to, in the fashion of the day. Capt. Dean also brought home thirteen sets of China ware to order, for such families as could afford and thought proper to indulge in such luxuries.*

These articles were so much valued that they have passed from mothers to daughters, down to the present time; and, though much broken and scattered, are objects of curiosity, not only from the associations connected with this singular voyage, but as showing the form and style of China ware sixty years ago. A set which belonged to Capt. Johnson, a revolutionary veteran, whose house stood with its gable to the street, on the corner of South Pearl and Howard streets, where the Centre Market now stands, was divided among his descendants. One set, however, has been preserved nearly complete, and is in the possession of Mrs. Abraham Ten Eyck, in Broadway. These sets being mostly bought to order had the initials of the owners' names gilded upon each piece.

It was a matter of surprise to the natives and Europeans in those seas, to see so small a vessel arrive from a clime so remote from China, and gave them an exalted conception of the enterprise of the citizens of the United States. At some of the ports where the Experiment *touched, it is said that she was an object of alarm to the inhabitants, who mistook her for a tender to a fleet of men-of-war. She returned to New York Sunday, April 22, 1787, without the loss of a man during the voyage. On her arrival she was visited by at least two-thirds of the citizens, it is said; very few of whom had expected her return. Capt. Dean made several voyages to China subsequently, when the famous merchant Howqua formed so favorable an opinion of him that he was accustomed to send over a chest of black tea occasionally for the captain, long after the latter had discontinued his voyages. Capt. Dean died in New York, a few years since, age 85, at the house of Mr. Roderick Sedgwick.*

References: Joel Munsell, *The Annals of Albany*, 10 volumes (Albany, 1850–1859); manifest of the sloop *Experiment*, New-York Historical Society.

B8 *Cup and Saucer*, c. 1786
Diameter of saucer: 4⅞ inches
Loan: Albany Institute of History and Art (X40.700.562AB)

This cup and saucer are decorated in an unpretentious "country" style which shows no sign of the use of the border patterns favored by 1790 on Chinese porcelain for the American market. The green and lav-

B8

ender looped floral band and central flower roundel are similar to the Ten Eyck bowl (cat. B9).

The saucer has a label reading "Brought by Capt. Dean 1777." Although the date is clearly wrong (1787 might be the proper date), all other factors are appropriate.

B9 *Small Bowl*, c. 1786–1790
Diameter: 5½ inches
Loan: Albany Institute of History and Art (x40.700.657)

This small bowl also fits the criteria for possibly being part of the cargo of the *Experiment*. It is of modest design of the early American period, but with feathery festoons below a blue enamel and star border. It also has an unusual "open flower" roundel in lavender on either side. The Albany Institute's files record that it came from the collection of Peter G. Ten Eyck and the extract from the *Annals of Albany* quoted above mentions that in 1850 there was "one set...nearly complete...in the possession of Mrs. Abraham Ten Eyck, in Broadway." She was the mother of Peter G. Ten Eyck. (Not illustrated.)

B10 *Mug*, c. 1786–1790
Height: 5⅞ inches
Loan: Sleepy Hollow Restorations, Tarrytown, New York (v.c. 58.199)

This plain, cylindrical mug with a serpent-headed handle is decorated with *famille rose* flowers in the style of European country ware. The mug was a modest and inexpensive drinking vessel of a type which would have been in everyday use in a moderately affluent family. Robert Bolton reported that Captain Dean of the *Experiment* brought porcelain from China for General Pierre Van Cortlandt (1721–1813). The mug is of exactly the style of porcelain brought back by Captain Dean. Mrs. Robert P. Browne of Garden City returned the mug to Van Cortlandt Manor in 1958.

Reference: Joseph T. Butler, *Sleepy Hollow Restorations: A Cross Section of the Collections* (Tarrytown: Sleepy Hollow Restorations Collection, 1983), 95.

B10

B11 *Saucer*, c. 1785–1790
Diameter: 4⅞ inches
Loan: Sleepy Hollow Restorations, Tarrytown, New York (v.c. 58.204)

This saucer is of the type imported into

America during the first five years of the American China trade. The pink scale decoration at the rim and the pink flower sprays are typical. This piece is a further example of porcelain of the type that Captain Dean probably brought back on the *Experiment* and may have been one of the pieces that Bolton mentioned as "brought ...from China for Gen. Pierre Van Cortlandt."

B11

B12

BI2 *Beaker Vase*, c. 1785
Height: 10⅞ inches
Loan: New York State, Office of Parks, Recreation, and Historic Preservation, Bureau of Historic Sites. Clermont State Historic Site, Taconic State Park Region (CL. 1983.347A)

This beaker vase, originally from a garniture of five pieces, is decorated in underglaze blue with bouquets of *famille rose* flowers. Garnitures of this style were very popular in the 1780s and 1790s. This is exactly the type of garniture which Chancellor Robert R. Livingston (1746–1813) would have purchased shortly after the opening of the American China trade to furnish his new house. It is known that he received pieces from the cargo of the *Experiment*. This might be one of them.

BI3

BI3 *Beaker Vase*, c. 1785
Height: 11⅜ inches
Loan: New York State, Office of Parks, Recreation, and Historic Preservation,

Bureau of Historic Sites. Clermont State Historic Sites, Taconic State Park Region. (CL. 1983.348AB)

Of very similar shape and date to the previous vase, this too would have been part of a garniture. The more formal pedestal and basket of flowers replaces the bouquet of *famille rose* flowers. The vase was probably purchased about 1786 by Chancellor Livingston for the rebuilt Clermont.

BI4

BI4 *Small Platter*, c. 1785
Diameter: 9⅞ inches
Loan: Albany Institute of History and Art (x40.700.34)

This platter with a crimson trellis border and shield with floral surround, painted with "C" over "D.T.B.," belonged to Dirck Ten Broeck (1765–1832) and his wife, Cornelia Stuyvesant, daughter of Petrus Stuyvesant and Margaret Livingston. Ten Broeck was the only son of General Abraham Ten Broeck of Albany. He studied law and entered politics in Albany county. Later he served in the New York Assembly and became speaker of the House. He practiced law in New York City and was married in September 1785.

The Ten Broecks were a prominent Albany family for three centuries. Dirck Wessels Ten Broeck, the seventeenth-century progenitor, was an early Indian trader active in the civic and mercantile life of Beverwyck.

BI5 *Punch Bowl*, c. 1785–1788
Diameter: 14¾ inches
Loan: Anonymous

BI5

A great many fine bowls depict the thirteen factories along the waterfront at Canton. These are known as Hong bowls. The earliest were made with a single panel scene about 1765. By 1785 the design was continuous around the entire bowl. Most examples are in polychrome. This one is well painted and very similar to the bowl in the Mottahedeh Collection.

Interest centers on the flags being flown. While the Mottahedeh bowl was made about 1785 and has no American flag, this is an early example of one with an American flag. The position of the flag is not correct, since it actually flew next to the Swedish flag. Nevertheless, although flags have been added to Hong bowls, this one appears on close examination to be original. It may therefore be the earliest type of bowl decorated with an American flag, even before the United States had its own factory.

The *Empress of China*'s cargo included one tub in Captain Green's private cargo which contained "4 Factory Painted Bowles @5½ [dollars] each." It seems unlikely that they would have had an American flag, but if they did, it would have been added hastily wherever there was space, as in this case on the veranda of the British East India Co. factory.

Reference: For an illustration of the Mottahedeh bowl together with other recorded examples, see David Howard and John Ayers, *China for the West* (London: Sotheby, Parke Bernet, 1978), 209.

B16 *Porcelain of the Society of the Cincinnati*

Most of the porcelain made for members of the Society of the Cincinnati resulted from two visits to China by Major Samuel Shaw. Shaw's first voyage was as supercargo on the *Empress of China*, and his journal contains the following entry:

> There are many painters in Canton, but I was informed that not one of them possesses a genius for design. I wished to have something emblematic of the institution of the order of the Cincinnati executed upon a set of porcelain. My idea was to have the American Cincinnatus, under the conduct of Minerva, regarding fame . . . and furnished the painter with a copy of the emblem, which I had in my possession . . . The best of his essays I preserved, as a specimen of Chinese excellence in design, and it is difficult to regard it without smiling.

Samuel Shaw returned with the *Empress of China*, but he left instructions that further cargo which was not ready should follow on the *Pallas* (see cat. B2 and B3).

Following Major Shaw's return to China, he supervised the manufacture of a number of tea services as gifts for friends who were members of the Order. In all, two punch bowls and thirteen services, three for dinner and ten for tea or coffee, of Cincinnati porcelain are known. There may well have been more of each; from time to time claims have been made that Colonel Stevens ordered other bowls for his friends and that Samuel Shaw gave other tea services to members.

There is no record of the date when the punch bowls were ordered. From the style of decoration inside the rim of the Stevens bowl, it must have been about 1790. Although it is the less spectacular of the two, the painting is finer. The Stevens bowl is signed by the Chinese artist "Synchong," as on General Morton's bowl (cat. c71). Synchong's best known period is c. 1800–1815. Nevertheless, it is the opinion of this cataloguer that the date of the bowl is earlier.

The full list of original owners as presently known, with probable date of making the porcelain, is as follows:

George Washington	Dinner Service	1785	Exhibit B3
Henry Lee	Dinner Service	1785	Exhibit B3
Samuel Shaw	Tea Service	1789–1790	Exhibit B17
	Dinner Service	1789–1790	
David Townsend	Tea Service	1789–1790	
Benjamin Lincoln	Tea Service	1789–1790	
William Eustis	Two Tea Services	1789–1790	
William Lithgo	Tea Service	1789–1790	
Constant Freeman	Tea Service	1789–1790	
Henry Knox	Tea Service	1789–1790	
Andrew Craigie	Tea Service	1789–1790	
Ebenezer Stevens	Punch Bowl	c.1790	Exhibit B18
Richard Varick	Punch Bowl	c.1800	Exhibit B19

B17

BI9

References: Josiah Quincy, ed., *The Journal of Major Samuel Shaw, The First American Consul at Canton* (Boston: 1847), 198–199; John Quentin Feller, "China Trade Porcelain Decorated with the Emblem of the Society of the Cincinnati," *The Magazine ANTIQUES* 118, no. 4 (Oct. 1980), 460–468; John Quentin Feller, "The Society of the Cincinnati," Bicentennial Exhibit at the Peabody Museum, Salem, Massachusetts, May to September 1983.

BI7 *Part Tea and Chocolate Service*, c. 1788

Height of chocolate pot (illustrated): 8½ inches
Collection of The New-York Historical Society, part of a group of seventeen pieces (1972.11 A–Q), gift of Miss Frances Jay, Mrs. Alexander Duer Harvey, Mrs. Lloyd Kirkham Garrison, and Mrs. Lawrence W. Fox, in memory of Mrs. Pierre Jay (*née* Louisa Shaw Barlow) by her children.

This porcelain forms the most complete set for chocolate and tea bearing the badge of the Society of the Cincinnati. The decoration is plain with feathery wave patterns. Each piece has the emblem and the initials "S.S." for Samuel Shaw. The badge painted on the chocolate pot is exceptionally large.

This chocolate and tea service, which

Shaw did not order on his first voyage, has exactly the same decoration as that ordered in 1789 or 1790 for David Townsend, William Eustis, Benjamin Lincoln, and others. Whether Shaw ordered his service, which is larger than the others, on a previous journey is uncertain.

Samuel Shaw was the first American consul in Canton. He died in 1794. His porcelain descended successively to his nephew, Robert Gould Shaw (1776–1853), and Robert's eldest son, Francis George Shaw (1809–1882). Francis's four daughters, including Ellen Shaw who married Francis C. Barlow, then divided the service. Ellen Shaw was the mother of Louisa Shaw Barlow, whose daughters donated seventeen pieces of the service to The New-York Historical Society in 1972.

BI8 *Punch Bowl*, c. 1790

Diameter: 16 inches
Loan: The Metropolitan Museum of Art, on loan from Mrs. Charles A. Pfeffer.

This magnificent punch bowl, decorated *en grisaille* with fine trellis work on the rim, has the exact reproduction of the certificate of membership of Ebenezer Stevens (1751–1823) of the Society of the Cincinnati painted

around the rim of the exterior. The rim and foot are banded with silver because of early breaks. The text on the bowl, dated December 1785, reads:

Be it known that Ebenezer Stevens, Lieutenant Colonel of the late 2nd Regiment of Artillery is a member of the Society of the Cincinnati instituted by the Officers of the American Army at the Period of its Dissolution as well to commemorate the great Event which gave Independence to North America... by order H. Knox Secretary. G. Washington President.

This is said to be one of a number of such bowls ordered by Ebenezer Stevens himself, but only one of a later date for Colonel Richard Varick is known (cat. BI9). After the war, Colonel Stevens was owner or part owner of a number of ships trading to Canton. He was a member of the New York Society of the Cincinnati. The bowl is signed by Synchong, who was at the height of his reputation in Canton about 1800. A much later bowl made for General Morton in 1812 has Synchong's name (presumably then the owner of the studio) as well as the actual painter (cat. C71).

Although later dates have been given to this bowl, there seems no reason why it should not have been made before 1790. Ebenezer Stevens was later major general, commanding all New York artillery, and as such was the senior officer of General Morton. (Not illustrated.)

BI9 *Punch Bowl*, c. 1790–1800

Diameter: 16 inches
Loan: Morristown National Historic Park, gift of the Washington Association, 1933

This is the most magnificent of the punch bowls connected with the Society of the Cincinnati. Within the rim, it has a band of decoration of red and blue enamel with a gilt vine edge. On the exterior, below a blue enamel band with stars, is painted the full certificate of membership of the Society for Colonel Richard Varick. To the left of the inscription is a polychrome enamel scene of the figure of Liberty as Cincinnatus holding the American flag and with the American eagle. Gilt bolts of lightning

BI9

BI9

there is no reason why this should not be one of the bowls reputed to have been ordered by Ebenezer Stevens.

Richard Varick served as military secretary to General Schuyler, but his military career was blighted when, after being appointed aide to Benedict Arnold at West Point in 1780, the latter's treason was uncovered. He asked for and was given a court of enquiry which acquitted him with honor. He was still an object of suspicion, however, until General Washington himself appointed Varick as his confidential secretary in charge of his correspondence. In 1784 Varick became Recorder of New York City, in 1787 Speaker of the New York Assembly, and Mayor of New York in 1789, which office he held until 1801.

B20 *Teabowl and Saucer,* c. 1785–1788
Diameter of saucer: 3½ inches
Loan: The Metropolitan Museum of Art, Rogers Fund, 1935. (36.51.1); bookplate, The Metropolitan Museum of Art, gift of William E. Bailey, 1920

This service is decorated with wavy dotted lines, flower sprays, and a finely patterned border. The teabowl has the crest of a lion rampant holding a spray of flowers and a monogram, while larger pieces of the service have a complete armorial. The design is copied from the bookplate of James H. Giles of New York and was engraved by Robert Montgomery, who was working about 1783. It includes an American flag as a patriotic gesture.

It is clear that a bookplate was sent to China for copying. The armorials are of the Giles family, originally of Bowden in Devon, England. James Giles was a lieutenant in the artillery during the American Revolution.

repel the British Lion and the figure of Britannia. On the right of the certificate is the Angel of Fame holding the seal of the Society. This detail is taken from the elaborate engraving of Robert Scott of Philadelphia. The wording of the certificate is very similar to that on Colonel Stevens's bowl, but records the membership of "Richard Varick, Esq." The quality of lettering, is not so fine. The certificate is signed "H. Knox Secretary G. Washington President."

The date of this bowl has always aroused some discussion, but this writer considers that there is no reason why it need be after 1790, and that it is certainly not after 1800. Colonel Richard Varick (1753–1831) was also a member of the New York Society and

References: For an illustration of an earlier service made for the English Giles family, see David Sanctuary Howard, *Chinese Armorial Porcelain* (London: Faber and Faber, 1974), 440. See fragment exhibited. See also, Clare Le Corbeiller, "China Trade Armorial Porcelain in America," *The Magazine ANTIQUES* 112, no. 6 (December, 1977), 1124–1129.

B20 SAUCER

B21

B22

B20 BOOKPLATE

B21 *Teabowl,* c. 1785–1790
Diameter: 3½ inches
Loan: Sleepy Hollow Restorations, Tarry-town, New York (v.c. 58.201)

This is a delicately painted teabowl with a wavy rim and a small stylized scene. A feathery band of decorations is within the rim of the cup. The bowl is of European quality of the late 1780s; the decoration is derived ultimately from Meissen styles of the late 1770s. It indicates an unusually wide choice of style for pieces associated with the American market, and may have come in one of the first cargoes after 1785.

The teabowl has a long history at Van Cortlandt Manor.

B22 *Teabowl,* c. 1785–1790
Diameter: 3⅜ inches
Loan: Sleepy Hollow Restorations, Tarry-town, New York (v.c. 58.202/203)

This teabowl, one of a pair at Van Cort-landt Manor, combines a feathery floral rim design typical of the late 1780s with the simple blue enamel band and stars which were popular in the early 1790s. This is not a common design, and owes something to English creamware with molded rims dat-ing from the late 1780s. The flower spray is more standard.

B23 *Plate*, c. 1785–1790
Diameter: 7½ inches
Loan: Anonymous

This plate is from one of two very similar services. It has a somewhat complex border of blue enamel, gilding, and stars. In the center there is an armorial, "Or, a lion rampant vert." The crest may be a "reindeer's head between two wings" (or a "griffin's head and wings"). Below the arms is the single word "Morgan." Very similar arms were confirmed to the Morgans of Flushing in 1683 and of Boston in 1636. John and Elias Morgan were half brothers and two prominent Hartford merchants about 1790. A relative, another John Morgan, was the carpenter on board the *Empress of China* on its maiden voyage. According to the family biographer, this service returned in the cargo in 1785, although the style is more appropriate to 1790 and it may have returned on a later voyage.

References: Clare Le Corbeiller, "China Trade Armorial Porcelain in America," *The Magazine ANTIQUES* 112, no. 6 (December, 1977), 1124–1129. Nathaniel Morgan, *A History of James Morgan...and his Descendants* (Hartford: 1869), 92–93

B24 *Plate*, c. 1785–1790
Diameter: 9⅝ inches
Loan: The Metropolitan Museum of Art, gift of Charles K. Davis, 1949 (48.172.3)

This plate is part of a service identical with the previous exhibit, except that the name "Elias Morgan" appears below the arms. Family tradition asserts that this was the second of the two services, and that it was made about two years after the one above.

B25 *Pudding Plate*, c. 1785–1790
Diameter: 6¼ inches
Loan: The Metropolitan Museum of Art, gift of Ginsburg and Levy, Inc., 1956

This wavy-edged small plate with enamel border and leafy waving band at rim has an armorial in the center with a heart be-low a chevron within a floral mantling and a motto.

These are the arms of Elias Boudinot (1740–1821) of New Jersey. Elias, a lawyer, represented New Jersey in Congress and was its president in 1782. He was a friend of George Washington, supplying him with cider from his estate in Elizabeth. Elias was son of Elias (trained as a silversmith but later in the business of copper mining) who was born in New York, whence his Huguenot grandfather had emigrated from La Rochelle via London and died there in 1702.

Reference: Clare Le Corbeiller, "China Trade Armorial Porcelain in America," *The Magazine ANTIQUES* 112, no. 6 (December, 1977), 1124–1129.

B26 *Pair of Pudding Plates*, c. 1790
Diameter: 6½ inches
Loan: National Society of Colonial Dames, Van Cortlandt Mansion

Decorated with two bands of underglaze blue trellis work with spearhead borders, these plates have a shield on mantling with the initials "H.A.W." and the crest of a lion's head at the center. The initials belong to Henry A. Wright, whose origins are uncertain. The service has a long history in the Van Cortlandt family at Van Cortlandt Mansion.

B23

B24

B25

B26

B27 SAUCER

B28

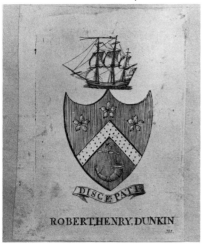

B27 BOOKPLATE

B27 *Plate,* c. 1790
Diameter of plate: 7½ inches
Loan: Anonymous

This service has an underglaze blue trellis border and central arms of a style popular in England and Scotland at the end of the eighteenth century. The arms are those of the Duncan family of Scotland.

The service has belonged to the Dunkin family of Philadelphia and New York since the late eighteenth century, and these are the arms used on Dunkin silver and their bookplate. The bookplate (illustrated) is designed exactly as the Chinese service and probably acted as an original sent to

China. It is just possible, however, that the bookplate was copied from the service.

Robert Henry Dunkin, who married Elizabeth Watkins of Harlem, New York, in 1792 and had been brought up by his probably widowed mother in Philadelphia, always understood that his father was an officer in the Royal Navy. Although a Robert Dunkin is in the naval records until 1775, there is no mention of him after that date. The belief also persisted that they were descendants of the Duncans of Scotland and not the Irish family of Dunkin which bore different arms.

Robert Henry died in 1808, leaving an only daughter, Ann, who married John S. Van Rensselaer of Albany in 1816. The porcelain is recorded in an inventory of that family of 1835.

Because of the bookplate, it is clear that the Dunkin family owned this service in the late eighteenth century. The story is an excellent example of how American families, though free politically, clung tenaciously to family histories in Europe and even assumed armorials to which they may have had only the slightest claim or none at all. In no way, however, does this alter the interesting provenance of this porcelain in the hands of a New York family.

The bookplate is of Robert Henry Dunkin before 1796.

B28 *Oval Pierced Basket Stand,* c. 1785–1790
Length: 8¼ inches
Loan: National Society of Colonial Dames, Van Cortlandt Mansion

Pierced or reticulated fruit baskets belonged to dessert services which had plates with similar borders. This basket has an enameled, patterned rim and a spray of finely enameled blue flowers in the center. On the reverse the National Society of Colonial Dames has placed a label reading "Presented by Mrs. F. M. Goddard (about 1896) Gift. Chinese Lowestoft ware used by Mrs. Robsands during the occupation of New York by the British and given by her daughter to Mrs. Goddard." The stand was probably made shortly after the British occupation of New York, although it may possibly have been made earlier. It is much more likely that Mrs. Robsands had a mixed set of Chinese porcelain at the time to which she added some replacement pieces, including this one, at the beginning of the American China trade.

B29 *Punch Bowl,* c. 1790
Diameter: 13 inches
Loan: National Society of Colonial Dames, 215 East 71st Street, New York City

This punch bowl may be unique, but it was almost certainly made for the American market and has a considerable history in New York. Formal floral swags decorate the outside. Each side bears a finely painted oval vignette of a volcanic Pacific island. The inside has a band of blue enamel with stars at the rims and an unidentified armorial in an oval panel.

Ships of the British merchant fleet crossed the Pacific only on the rarest of occasions, while the route was a common one for American vessels. The volcanic island must certainly be a copy of a contemporary engraving. No standard work records the armorial, but it is nearest to the arms of Gifford. At least one piece of a dinner service in this style and with these arms has survived. It was not uncommon to have a dinner service with special decoration on either punch bowls or mugs. (Shown on p. 84.)

B29

B29A

In later life he resided at 34 Wall Street. He received a patent in 1803 for a device for use on ships "for extracting pure, wholesome and fresh water from water of the Ocean, by means of evaporation and condensation."

B30 *Pair of Plates*, c. 1790
Diameter: 9¾ inches
Loan: New York State, Office of Parks, Recreation, and Historic Preservation, Bureau of Historic Sites, Clermont State Historic Site, Taconic State Park Region (CL 1981 43 and CL 1981 46)

Decorated in an underglaze blue, these plates belong to a small set. The style is almost exactly the same as the service originally ordered by Thomas Fitzhugh, c. 1780. Fitzhugh was a director of the British East India Company and the style today is named after him. It would have been natural to find this style in stock in Canton in the late 1780s, and natural too that Robert R. Livingston should have wished to order the latest styles of porcelain when he rebuilt Clermont after it was destroyed by the British in 1777 (see cat. A11). The service was almost certainly delivered by 1790.

Reference: For an illustration of one of Thomas Fitzhugh's dishes, c. 1780, see David Sanctuary Howard, *Chinese Armorial Porcelain* (London: Faber and Faber, 1974), 52.

B30

B29a *Punch Bowl*, c. 1790
Diameter: 15½ inches
Loan: The Metropolitan Museum of Art, bequest of Mrs. Edith Pryor, 1935 (35.112)

An underglaze blue trellis and spearhead design decorates the rim of this large punch bowl. A floral swag and tassel pattern embellishes the rim decoration. A husk chain encircles the foot of the bowl. On each side of the bowl there is a merchant ship, flying an American flag, very similar to the *Empress of China* and the *Grand Turk* (cat. B1).

The bowl bears the initials "J.L." It was made for John Lamb, a prominent New York citizen and former leader of the Sons of Liberty. In the aftermath of the battles of Lexington and Concord, Lamb urged New Yorkers on April 23, 1775, to defend the "injured rights and liberties of America."

B32

B31 *Pair of Plates*, c. 1790–1810
Diameter: 9¼ inches
Loan: Joseph C. Cockrell, Jr.

These plates are decorated in an underglaze blue exactly like the original service made for Thomas Fitzhugh. The central medallion bears the initials "W.C.R." The service is said to have been made for William C. Rhinelander of New York. This is presumably William Copeland Rhinelander, who first appears in the New York directory in 1814. Rhinelander married Mary Rogers and died in 1878. The service may have belonged to Rhinelander if it was a present at his coming of age or an early wedding present. It is also possible, however, that the porcelain was made to the order of his father, William Rhinelander, who had married Mary Robert and died in 1825. The estate of the late Philip Rhinelander II contained pieces, although much of his porcelain had no initials and had been bought to make up a service, a very common practice. (Not illustrated.)

B32 *Milk Jug*, c. 1780
Height: 4¾ inches
Loan: Abigail Adams Smith Museum, New York City

The remaining pieces of the service of which this jug is a part are decorated with a roundel with pink enamelled ribbon bow above and two floral sprays below. On the roundel is a gilt flower spray. This type of decoration more usually enclosed initials.

The service first belonged to President John Adams, the second president of the United States, and passed to his daughter, Abigail. She married William Stephen Smith, who later lived at the house now on 61st Street, New York City, where the service still is. It is one of two tea and coffee services made for the Adams family (see cat. c36).

B33 *Sugar Bowl Stand and Teabowl*, c. 1790
Diameter of sugar bowl stand: 6⅜ inches
Loan: Dr. Robert S. Beekman

An unusual and attractive engrailed gilt border with lavender spearheads decorates pieces of this service at the rim. Green and gold dots decorate the well. Each piece has a bright blue mantle with ermine lining and the initials "S.R." in gold on a shield.

The service was made for Samuel Riker, born in 1743 of a Dutch family. The Rikers came to New Amsterdam from Holland in 1638 and received a patent from Governor Stuyvesant for Hewlett's Island, since known as Riker's Island. Samuel Riker took an active role against the Crown during the American Revolution and had to flee his home in Newtown, Long Island, when British troops occupied it.

In 1769 Riker married Anna, daughter of Joseph Lawrence. They had nine children. The Rikers may have purchased this service to celebrate their twentieth wedding anniversary. Samuel died in 1823.

B33

The First Century of the American China Trade, 1790–1880

CI *Teabowl*, c. 1790

Diameter: 3½ inches
Loan: The Metropolitan Museum of Art,
Rogers Fund 1935 (35.13)

It is surprising and sad that neither the two tea services with the full arms of the State of New York nor the coffee service bearing the arms of the Commonwealth of Pennsylvania have provenances. If a merchant's book or captain's log contains the answer, it has not yet been found.

This teabowl has a simple blue enamel band at the rim, with stars, engrailed gilding, and a blue and gold husk chain. The arms are well painted, but are not quite accurate, as they are correctly "blazoned" or described: "From behind a mountain a rising sun." Crest: "An eagle with wings addorsed holding in its dexter claw a ball." Supporters: "Dexter, Justice holding in her hand a fasces and in her sinister hand a rod. Sinister, Liberty holding in her sinister hand a staff, on the top of which a cap of Liberty." Motto: "Excelsior."

There are a number of discrepancies between this description and the painting, most notably that the sun appears over a level plain. A great number of pseudo armorials with initials and gilt sprays immortalize the style and design (cats. c5–c30). The best have the motto and are otherwise very similar to this.

c2 *Part Tea Service*, c. 1790

Loan: Cup and saucer, The Metropolitan Museum of Art, Harris Brisbane Dick Fund, 1936; Commission from Governor George Clinton to James Lyons, Collection of The New-York Historical Society

This service, with the full arms of New York, is in most respects similar to CI except that the rim design is a plain, wavy blue enamel band. The shield of the armorial, however, is quite different in style. On the shield there are a number of Italianate, pinnacle-like hillocks, from behind which the sun is rising. The armorial of the state differs from the one with a single

mountain used by Governor George Clinton on his commission to James Lyons, June 16, 1778 (exhibited but not illustrated).

It is not known whether any purchasing link connects the two services with pseudo arms and Latin inscriptions, "I. Victorio," (cat. c23) and "Prescia," (cat. c22). The motto, "Excelsior," is clearly painted.

c3 *Porcelain with Initials and the Pseudo Arms of New York State*

We will probably never know who suggested using the full arms of the State of New York on porcelain, and substituting initials and flower sprays for "the sun over a mountain" on the shield. Following the success of the Cincinnati porcelain, however, by 1790 orders had been given to copy the eagle and shield found on the Massachusetts copper cent of 1787 onto porcelain, and to use initials on that shield. Perhaps a year later, New York State arms were used

CI

C2

in the same way. There is only one known piece with both the eagle and the New York arms, a beaker vase, part of a garniture, at The New-York Historical Society (cat. c16).

The pieces with the arms of New York were almost certainly made for residents of the state. In addition to the comparatively small number of services which were specially ordered with the initials of families, a greater number with sprays of gilt flowers was shipped for general sale.

Twenty-four initialed coffee or tea services—but no dinner services—have been found. Of these, only four have been identified, including two from the same family. It is hoped that the following list will produce further identifications. The initials are not necessarily of one person, as the Greenwood services show, since frequently the husband's and wife's initials were both included. Occasionally, the family initial was in the center, further complicating identification.

Among the armorials there are a number of variants. The best, and possibly the earliest, include the motto "Excelsior" on the motto scroll. The quality of the painting varies and there are a number of different border patterns. The supporters vary considerably. Justice has only the traditional sword as well as the scales of justice in one case (cat. c29). In most cases two small national shields hang beneath the arms. In one case the crest alone is used (cat. c28).

Porcelain with initials and the pseudo arms of the State of New York was made for only two decades, 1790–1810. A finely painted service in sepia with Liberty seated may have been the last example.

c4 *A Check List of Porcelain with Initials and the Pseudo Arms of the State of New York*

Initials	Family Name	Piece	Owner	Exhibited	Sale
JCB		Garniture	Winterthur	c15	
MAJC		Saucer	Sotheby's		Garbisch
MAJC		Small plate	Reeves Collection	c29	
MAJC		Saucer	Sotheby's		2/3/79
WRC		Saucer dish	Harriman	c8	
WRC		Cup and saucer	Henry Ford Museum	c8	
WRC		Coffee pot	Gill	c8	
TD		Teapoy	Metropolitan Museum	c11	
EF	Eliza Fisher	Pair of bowls	Gill	c30	
EF	Eliza Fisher	Saucer	Metropolitan Museum	c30	
EF	Eliza Fisher	Cake plate	Winterthur	c30	
JC and MF		Coffee cup	N.-Y.H.S.	c20	
GDG		Teabowls and saucer		Christie's	3/23/82
GDG		Bouillon bowl		Sotheby's	Garbisch
GDG		Coffee cup and saucer	Winterthur	c5	
MATG		Cup and saucer		*	
JEG	J. E. Greenwood	Part service	N.-Y.H.S.	c27	
JEG	J. E. Greenwood	Pair of urns	N.-Y.H.S.	c28	
LCH		Flagon	China Trade Museum	c31	
FJDCL		Sugar bowl	N.-Y.H.S.	c21	
FJDCL		Saucer	Albany Institute	c21	
MGL	Livingston (?)	Teapot	Albany Institute	c13	
MGL	Livingston (?)	Hot water jug	Sotheby's		11/27/79
IBM		Coffee pot	Harriman	c14	
JDCP		Bowl and saucer	N.-Y.H.S.	c7	
Prescia		Cream jug	Metropolitan Museum	c22	
Prescia		Saucer dish	N.-Y.H.S.	c22	
AMR		Sugar bowl, cover	Gill	c9	
IADR		Teapot	Gill	c12	
HCDPR	H. and C. Rutgers	Bowl and saucer	N.-Y.H.S.	c6	
HCDPR	H. and C. Rutgers	Oval stand	Sotheby's		Garbisch
JSHR		Plate	Harriman	c25	
JSHR		Plate	N.-Y.H.S.	c25	
JS		Teapot	Gill	c26	
JS (different style)		Mug	Gill	c10	
JST		Bowl and saucer	N.-Y.H.S.	c24	
JST		Bowl	Gill	c24	
I. Victorio		Sugar bowl	Harriman	c23	
I. Victorio		Coffee pot, bowl, saucer	N.-Y.H.S.	c23	
Umor		Teapot stand	Sotheby's		1/23/81

*See John G. Philips, *China-Trade Porcelain: An Account of its Historical Background, Manufacture, and Decoration and a Study of the Helena Woolworth McCann Collection* (London, 1956).

c5 *Coffee Cup and Saucer*, c. 1785–1790

Diameter of saucer: 5½ inches
Owned by: Henry Francis du Pont Winterthur Museum. Catalogued, but not exhibited (m56.38.53 and m56.38.54)

This style of armorial porcelain, with tiny lappets in enamel at the rim and a wavy dotted line punctuated with small flower sprays, was popular in the British market. The pseudo arms of the State of New York have the initials "G.D.G." on the shield. These initials have not been identified.

c5

c6 *Teabowl and Saucer*, c. 1790

Diameter of saucer: 5½ inches
Diameter of cup: 3½ inches
Collection of The New-York Historical Society, gift of Waldron Phoenix Belknap, Jr. (1952.97A and 1952.97B)

This cup and saucer have an elaborate border decoration. The scalloped rim of the saucer has a blue enamel band with stars and spearheads inside. A worn gilt chain with a wavy line surrounds the arms. The shield contains the initials "H.C.D.P.R." within the pseudo arms of the State of New York. The service is said to have belonged to Catherine de Peyster, who married Henrick Rutgers in 1784. (Not illustrated.)

c7 *Pair of Teabowls and Saucers*, c. 1790

Diameter of cup: 3½ inches
Collection of The New-York Historical Society, gift of Mrs. L. V. Salon. (1953.15A; 1933.15B; 1933.16A; and 1933.16B)

These cups and saucers have more elaborate decoration than most with the pseudo arms of New York. The shaped rim of the

c9

c10

c7

C10 *Mug*, c. 1790
Height: 7⅛ inches
Loan: Peter Trowbridge Gill

This mug is decorated plainly, with a wavy band of blue enamel at the rim and a husk chain at the foot. The pseudo arms of New York have a shield with the initials "J.S." This may possibly have belonged to the same owner as a later service (cat. c26).

C11

CII

C12

saucer has a blue enamel band with stars and spearhead. Inside there is a worn gilt chain with a wavy line surrounding the arms. The shield has the initials "J.D.C.P." The original owner has not been identified.

c8 *Saucer Dish, Cup and Saucer, and Coffee Pot*, c. 1790
Diameter of saucer: 6⅜ inches
Loans: Saucer dish, Governor and Mrs. W. Averell Harriman; cup and saucer (illustrated), The Henry Ford Museum; coffee pot, Peter Trowbridge Gill
Photograph: Courtesy of The Henry Ford Museum

This saucer dish is from what is apparently the only service of New York arms with pink lappets on the rim and a gilt husk chain. The initials "W.R.C." on the shield of the State of New York have not been identified.

c9 *Sugar Bowl and Cover*, c. 1790
Height: 5⅞ inches
Loan: Peter Trowbridge Gill

This sugar bowl from a tea or coffee service is decorated with fine lines at the mouth and on the cover, and with the pseudo arms of New York. The shield is inscribed "A.M.R." It is not known to whom these initials belonged.

CII *Teapoy*, c. 1790
Height: 5¾ inches
Loan: The Metropolitan Museum of Art
(12.48.4)

With blue trellis band at the shoulder and
on the cover, this arched, rectangular teapoy, of a style which first became popular
c. 1770, is painted with the pseudo arms of
the State of New York. The initials on the
shield, "T.D.," have not been identified.
(Shown on p. 89.)

CI2 *Teapot*, c. 1790
Height: 6 inches
Loan: Peter Trowbridge Gill

This plain, drum-shaped teapot is decorated with a blue enamel band and stars.
A wavy line is at the base. The pseudo arms
of New York have the initials "I.A.D.R."
on the shield. The original owner has not
been identified. (Shown on p. 89.)

CI3 *Teapot and Sugar Bowl*, c. 1795
Height of sugar bowl: 5½ inches
Loans: Teapot, Albany Institute of History
and Art (1973.124); sugar bowl, Bernard and
S. Dean Levy, Inc., New York City

Decorated in a style appropriate to the end
of the eighteenth century, these pieces
have blue enamel and gold pattern bands,
and the pseudo arms of New York. The
shield bears the initials "M.G.L." The provenance of the service is not known, although
it may have been made for a member of the
Livingston family. There is no record of
such a service at Clermont.

CI4 *Coffee Pot*, c. 1795
Height: 9½ inches
Loan: Governor and Mrs. W. Averell Har-
riman

This coffee pot is decorated with a wavy,
blue enamel band and a husk chain. The
handle is twisted with vine leaf and berry
ends. The initials "I.B.M." or "J.B.M." on
the shield of the State of New York have
not been identified. A cup and saucer from
the same service are in the collections of
The New-York Historical Society (1952.129A
and 1952.129B)

CI5 *Garniture*, c. 1795
Height: 12¼ inches
Owned by: Henry Francis du Pont Win-
terthur Museum, Wilmington, Delaware.
Catalogued, but not exhibited

The most popular form of decorative porcelain of the eighteenth and early nineteenth
centuries was the garniture, or, to give it
its full name, *garniture de cheminée.* This bears
the pseudo arms of New York State and the
initials "J.C.B." on the shield. These initials
have not been identified. (Not illustrated.)

CI6 *Beaker Vase*, c. 1795
Height: 12¼ inches
Collection of The New-York Historical
Society, bequest of Mrs. J. Insley Blair,
(1952.114)

This cylindrical vase with a flaring lip,
probably one piece of a garniture of five, is
decorated simply with a blue enamel band
and two wavy lines at the rim and a husk
chain at the base. It is painted on one side
with the pseudo arms of the State of New
York with a gilt floral center, and on the
other side with an American eagle displayed in sepia. As far as is known, this is
the only piece of porcelain on which both
the New York arms and the American eagle
appear.

CI7 *Plate*, c. 1795
Diameter: 7¾ inches
Collection of The New-York Historical
Society, bequest of Mrs. J. Insley Blair
(1952.113)

With a blue enamel border, six small sprays
of flowers, and a husk chain, this plate also

CI4

CI3

CI6

C17

C19

C20

C18

and a blue enamel band at the rim, has the pseudo arms of New York containing a spray of flowers on the shield. The mug is typical of ware made for a market which was larger than that represented by the initialed services. Such porcelain was at its most popular between 1790 and 1800, and would certainly have been purchased by New York families.

has pseudo arms of New York with a floral spray in the center. Designed for customers who had not ordered specially, this porcelain was probably made after 1790 to meet popular demand.

C18 *Mug*, c. 1795
Height: 5 inches
Loan: Diplomatic Reception Rooms, U.S. Department of State, gift of Mrs. Foster Milliken (71.138)
Photograph: Diplomatic Reception Rooms, United States Department of State

This plain, cylindrical mug with gilt stars and a blue and gold husk chain at the base

C19 *Coffee Cup*, c. 1795
Height: 2⅝ inches
Loan: Peabody Museum, Salem, Massachusetts (E50, 472 A)

Here is a typical example from a coffee service with the pseudo arms of New York. A wavy blue enamel band and an alternate blue and gold husk chain decorate the cup. The shield has a gilt flower spray.

C20 *Coffee Cup*, c. 1795
Height: 2½ inches
Collection of The New-York Historical Society (1952.127)

This coffee cup from a service with the pseudo arms of the State of New York has a plain blue, wavy enamel band at the rim and a husk chain inside. It is unusual in that it has two pairs of initials, "J.C." and "M.F.," in gilding of a sketchy nature.

C21 *Sugar Bowl with Cover and Saucer*, c. 1795
Height of sugar bowl: 5½ inches
Diameter of saucer: 5½ inches
Loan: Saucer, Albany Institute of History and Art (1969.44.646), the gift of Mrs. Harry A. Popp in memory of her husband; sugar bowl with cover, collection of The New-York Historical Society, bequest of Mrs. J. Insley Blair (1952.115AB)

This sugar bowl and saucer belong to a service with molded and shaped rims. They are decorated with a blue enamel band and stars, a gilt trellis, and a husk chain. The pseudo arms of New York bear the initials "F.I.D.C.L." or "F.J.D.C.L." These initials have not been identified, but are almost certainly of a husband and wife.

C21

C22 *Milk Jug and Circular Dish*, c. 1795
Height of milk jug: 5⅜ inches
Diameter of dish: 8 inches
Loan: Milk jug, The Metropolitan Museum of Art (35.24.1); circular dish, Collection of The New-York Historical Society, bequest of Mrs. J. Insley Blair (1952.112)

The milk jug is a standard, helmet-shaped piece with molded bowl and foot, popular since about 1775. The milk jug and the circular dish both bear the pseudo arms of the State of New York containing the word "Prescia." The only border decoration is a repetitive band of blue and gold enamel. The inscription is unexplained.

C22

C23 *Part of Service*, c. 1795
Height of sugar bowl: 5¾ inches
Height of coffee pot: 8¼ inches
Loan: Governor and Mrs. W. Averell Harriman

The sugar bowl is decorated at the rim with blue enamel and wavy gilt lines typical of the last decade of the eighteenth century. Each coffee or tea service ordinarily contained only one sugar bowl and cover. The words "I. Victorio" on the shield of New York on this set have thus far remained unexplained. Perhaps they refer to the outcome of the War of Independence. The collection of The New-York Historical Society includes a coffee pot, tea bowl, and saucer from the same service.

C23

C24 *Teabowl*, c. 1800
Diameter: 4⅜ inches
Loan: Peter Trowbridge Gill

This teabowl with New York pseudo arms is in one of the best enameled styles brought from China. The rim inside the cup has a finely painted blue enamel and gold vine pattern. The initials on the shield of the pseudo arms of New York are "J.S.T." These initials have not been identified. A similar but larger bowl and saucer are in the collections of The New-York Historical Society (1952.110AB).

C24

C25 *Plate*, c. 1800
Diameter: 7½ inches
Loan: Governor and Mrs. W. Averell Harriman

This plate is well decorated with a broad blue enamel band with a gilt vine pattern on the rim and a husk chain within the well. The initials on the pseudo arms of New York are "J.S.H.R." This is the best painted pattern of pseudo arms of New York. The armorial also betrays this quality in the use of the motto, "Excelsior," instead of leaving a bare motto scroll. The New-York Historical Society owns a similar plate (1952.110C).

C25

C26 *Teapot*, c. 1800
Height: 6 inches
Loan: Peter Trowbridge Gill

This drum-shaped teapot, after a silver form, has a broad gold band at the lip and spout and the pseudo arms of New York. The initials "J.S." are on the shield. This teapot may have belonged to the same person who owned a mug also in this exhibition (cat. C10).

C26

C27 *Part of Tea Service*, c. 1800
Collection of The New-York Historical Society, bequest of Mary MacKaye Greenwood (1969 18 A–H)

In most respects this tea service, of which about twenty pieces remain, is characteristic of styles as early as 1790. Each piece has orange and gold lappet decoration at the rim and the pseudo arms of New York State with the initials "J.E.G." in the center. The spout of the teapot, however, is of a shape introduced about 1800. On this account, it seems more likely that the service dates from the very early nineteenth century.

The initials "J.E.G." are for Dr. and Mrs. John Greenwood of New York City. John Greenwood (1760–1819) was born in Boston. After serving in the army during the Revolution, he trained in 1785 as a dentist in New York City. He first advertised his practice the following year. In 1806 he traveled to France to learn his profession's latest methods. He is credited with being the inventor of the foot-powered drill and of the use of porcelain for artificial teeth. His most distinguished patient was President George Washington. Greenwood died at his Park Row house in New York City in 1819. His wife was Elizabeth (Weaver) Greenwood (1764–1831). The tea service was a bequest from a descendant. See also three pistol-handle vases with the same initials (cat c28).

C27

c28 *Three Urns*, c. 1800

Heights: 16 inches and 13 inches
Collection of The New-York Historical Society, bequest of Mary MacKaye Greenwood (1969.16A; 1969.16B; and 1969.17)

Two of these urns are of the same size; the third is smaller. As is the case with many large urns, these are painted predominantly in blue and orange, with marbled bases and some gilding. On each side there is a medallion with the initials "J.E.G." on the shield below the mantling. The crest only of the State of New York appears above the mantling. There is also a tea service with these initials on the pseudo arms of New York State (cat. c27). Like that service, these urns were made for John and Elizabeth Greenwood. These urns were a bequest from one of their descendants.

c29 *Small Plate*, c. 1800

Diameter: 6 inches
Loan: The Reeves Collection, Washington and Lee University, Lexington, Virginia. Governor Clinton Commission: Collection of The New-York Historical Society (not illustrated).

C28

C29

This plate is unusual in that it is probably from the only service with the arms of New York, either full or pseudo, which shows Justice with her sword. Early documents, such as the commission from Governor George Clinton to James Lyons, show the sword, but held in a hand across the body of Justice. The initials on the shield are "M.A.J.C." and have not been identified. The design was probably copied from a drawing sent to China at the beginning of the nineteenth century (see also cat. c30).

c30 *Pair of Teabowls and Saucer*, c. 1805

Diameter of saucer: 5½ inches
Loans: Teabowls, Peter Trowbridge Gill; saucer, The Metropolitan Museum of Art

These pieces are from a service the design of which follows a drawing of the New York arms entirely different from that used a decade earlier. The pieces are painted in sepia. The supporter, Liberty, is seated and Justice leans on the shield, which bears the initials "E.F.," rather than supporting it. The design is well painted. The motto, "Excelsior," is on the motto scroll. The initials are thought to be those of Eliza Fisher. They have sometimes been linked to Elizabeth Fisher, the second wife of Edward King, a New York banker, but this identification is impossible since she was not born until the 1830s. A cake plate from the same service is at the Henry du Pont Winterthur Museum (G56.46.100).

C31 *Jug and Cover*, c. 1805–1810
Height: 11¼ inches
Loan: China Trade Museum, Milton, Massachusetts

This flagon with cover has arms very similar to C30. Justice is more loosely dressed, however, and the initials "L.C.H." appear on the shield. A plain enamel band is at the rim. The initials have not been identified.

C32 *Map of the Pearl River*, 1794
Loan: Anonymous

When the *Empress of China* sailed in 1784, uncharted seas were a normal hazard of navigation and many a reef was discovered by the first ship that foundered on it. British cartographers were still mapping the mouth of the Pearl River and the channels to what is now Hong Kong in 1794 when Lord Macartney led an Embassy to China. The British squadron which remained near Macao spent much of its time surveying. Captain H. W. Parish's rough maps with soundings are still in existence.

American captains would have made use of charts of other nations in the early years of the China trade; this 1794 survey by Joseph Huddart of the upper reaches of the Pearl River from the Tiger's Mouth to Canton has full navigational directions with bearings and landmarks indicated. Such a map would have been essential to every American captain. This particular chart does not have a New York provenance.

C33 *Octant*, c. 1825
Dimensions of case: 13 inches by 11¾ inches (at lower end) by 5¼ inches
Loan: Francis H. Low

Octants like this one are navigational instruments for taking astronomical readings. They serve the same purpose as sextants, but the semicircular pieces, or arcs, at their bases describe one-eighth rather than one-sixth of a circle.

This octant is made of brass, ebony, and ivory. It dates from the early nineteenth century and is inscribed "J. Cox London." It fits in a baize-lined case decorated in gold with an eagle, which may be of different manufacture. The labels of three New York companies which repaired it at various times have also been affixed:

> John Bliss & Co., 110 Wall Street
> D. Eggert & Son, 209 Pearl Street
> Creighton and Black, 43 Fulton Street

The abbreviation "Capt." with a name erased appears on a ribbon by the shield on the case. Below are the words "Capt Charles P. Low/Ship N. B. Palmer." It is clear that the octant was not new when Captain Low purchased it.

Jacob A. Westervelt of New York built the clipper ship *N. B. Palmer*, which was launched in 1851, for A. A. Low & Bros., one of New York's most prominent China-trade firms. She was 214 feet in length and displaced 1490 tons. Because of its luxurious fittings, she was known as "Low's yacht" and the Low family regularly used her in their travels. Captain Charles Low, A. A. Low's youngest brother, was the only seaman in the family (see also cat. C107).

C34 *Octant*, c. 1850
Dimensions of case: 13 inches by 11¾ inches (at lower end) by 5¼ inches
Loan: Charles Burr Lamar

This octant, of very similar English make to the one that Captain Low used, is in a plain mahogany box. The instrument bears an engraved ivory label with the words, "CHADBURN OPTICIANS to H. R. H. PRINCE ALBERT, LIVERPOOL." Inside the box a label reads:

> DEMORY GRAY & W. D. ALDER
> Successors to Geo. C. A. Baker
> Chronometer manufacturers
> No. 62 South Street NEW YORK

The actual date of this instrument is narrowed by the mention of Prince Albert, Consort of Queen Victoria, who died in 1862. Captain Christian Jensen used this octant in New York's trade with China. He was the grandfather of the present owner.

C30

C31

c32

c33

c34

c35

c35 *Teapot*, c. 1795
Height: 6 inches
Loan: Brooklyn Museum, gift of Miss Susan D. Bliss (45.7.43)

This drum teapot is of a type common in Chinese porcelain from about 1780 onwards and copies the same form in silver. The spout, handle, and decoration are, however, of late eighteenth-century form, as is the eagle, which bears the initials "F.B."

There are very few eagles with New York provenance, although one must guess that a substantial number of pieces with this decoration were made for New York (see cat. c16 for a piece with both an eagle and the pseudo arms of New York). This piece was made for Frederick Bliss of New York.

c36 *Small Bowl*, c. 1795
Diameter: 4¾ inches
Loan: Abigail Adams Smith Museum, New York City

The few surviving pieces of this tea service include this bowl, probably made for sugar. Originally it must have had a cover. A blue enamel band with stars decorates the inside rim; outside, there is a wispy husk chain and a roundel with rays containing a gilt spray of flowers. There are no initials.

The service was made for President John Adams and was used together with an earlier service (cat. B32). It is possible, although there is no evidence, that the service was made at the time John Adams assumed the presidency in 1797. If this was the case, it was in keeping with later custom. The service descended to Adams's daughter, Abigail Adams Smith.

c36

c37 *Part of a Service*, c. 1795
Diameter of saucer: 5½ inches
Collection of The New-York Historical Society (1927.13–33; cup and saucer illustrated —1927.18A and 1927.18B)

This service is decorated with an elaborate blue enamel and gilt pattern. Stars are at the rim of the saucers; a pattern of linked diamonds is within. Two birds facing each other, each holding a spray of flowers, are in an oval cartouche at the center. They stand on a wreath as if representing a family crest.

Such pairs of lovebirds in the form of pseudo crests are common on Chinese porcelain services of this period. Captains and merchants may have brought them home to illustrate marital bliss. It has not ordinarily been possible to substantiate this speculation. This service, however, is known to have been given by Clarkson Crolius (1773–1843), later a well-known potter and politician in New York, to Elizabeth Meyer (d. 1858) at the time of their marriage in 1793.

The New-York Historical Society has other pieces from the Duykinck service (1923.32) and the Rutgers service (1952.97 A–B) bearing similar pseudo crests. (Shown on p. 96.)

c38 *Covered Sugar Bowl, Teabowl, and Saucer*, c. 1795
Diameter of saucer: 5⅜ inches
Loan: Brooklyn Museum, gift of Judge Townsend Scudder, in memory of his grandmother, Elizabeth Hewlett Scudder (51.159.43, 51.159.57 and 51.159.65)

A blue enamel band with stars encircles this cup and saucer, which belonged to a tea and dinner service. A gilt loop-and-tassel decoration hangs from the band. The shield, on ermine mantling, has the initials "J.H."

The initials belong to John Hewlett of Long Island, a man of considerable standing and means. When the British occupied New York in 1776, James Christie, the commissary general, sent at once to Hewlett "to procure and bring to me cattle and sheep for the use of the army.... You will also secure and seize for His Majesty's use all cattle and sheep belonging to Rebels." There is no indication how they fared.

Reference: *New-York Packet*, February 20, 1786.

c39 *Teabowl and Saucer*, c. 1795
Diameter of saucer: 6 inches
Loan: Albany Institute of History and Art (1960.81)

This cup and saucer are molded and fluted. Elaborate blue enamel and gilt trellis work decorate the rims. They bear the initials "C.F." for Cornelia Fondey (1763–1825), the daughter of William Hun and Sarah (De Forest) Hun of Albany. Cornelia Hun married John Fondey, Jr., of Albany in 1783.

John and Cornelia Fondey and their five living children are the subjects of Ezra Ames's famous group portrait, "The Fondey Family," painted in 1803 and now owned by the Albany Institute of History and Art.

c40 *Teabowl and Saucer*, c. 1795–1800
Diameter of teabowl: 4⅜ inches
Diameter of saucer: 6 inches
Loan: Sleepy Hollow Restorations, Tarrytown, New York (v.c. 58.141 and v.c. 58.142)

The molded teabowl and saucer are both slightly ribbed and scalloped at the rim. Decoration of blue enamel and gilding produces an unusual scallop and floret design. Small blue flower sprays accompany the band of blue enamel dots and a worn, wavy gilt line. This is one of four such cups and saucers at Van Cortlandt Manor, each with unusual decoration. In 1925, Mrs. Ann Stevenson Van Cortlandt

c38

c37

c39

presented the Daughters of the American Revolution Museum in Washington, D.C., with a similar teabowl and saucer.

c41 *Punch Bowl*, c. 1795
Diameter: 11 inches
Collection of The New-York Historical Society, gift of Samuel Hoffman (1925.28)

This punch bowl is of a style of Masonic ware popular in England. A number of similar bowls and mugs are in the Museum of the Grand Lodge of England in London. The decoration inside and outside the rim is typical of the period. The exterior and interior are painted with Masonic emblems.

The bowl belonged to Robert R. Livingston (1746–1813). Livingston, who had seen his home, Clermont, burned by the British in 1778 (cat. A11), was later chancellor

of New York State, the first United States minister of foreign affairs, and negotiator of the Louisiana Purchase.

Since this bowl was made when Chancellor Livingston was fifty, it may have been a birthday gift from fellow Masons. His portrait, attributed to Gilbert Stuart, may also have been painted that year.

c42 *Serving Platter*, c. 1795–1805
Length: 16 inches
Loan: Sleepy Hollow Restorations, Tarrytown, New York (v.c. 63.19)

This dish, painted in an underglaze blue, closely follows a style established in the 1780s and used on the first Cincinnati service (cat. B3). Its shaped corners and detailed scale, leaf, and butterfly border show care in painting which is lacking on most such

C4I (top)
A2I (left)
AI2 (bottom)
CI05B (top, right)
CI05C (bottom, right)

C121 (top)

C21 (left)

C99A (bottom)

c132 (top, left)

c132 (top, right)

c34 (bottom, right)

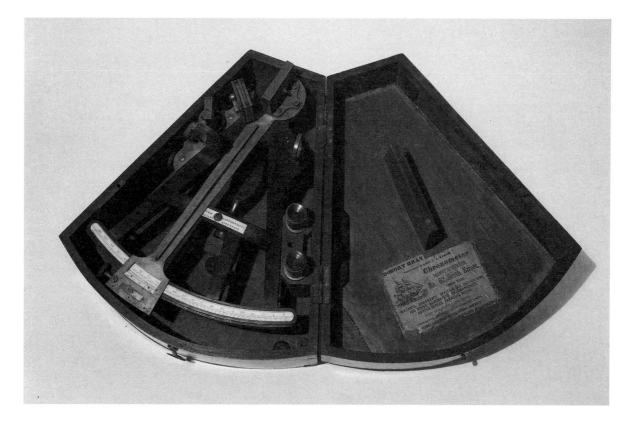

C104 (right)

C102 (far right)

C103 (below, left)

C108 (below, right)

C105A (below, far right)

c66

C40

C41

C42

C43

C44

underglaze blue ware after 1810. The pagodas and the river scene are painted with more than usual perspective.

The platter formed part of the bequest of Miss Elizabeth Van Cortlandt Baldwin of Baltimore, Maryland, to Van Cortlandt Manor, where it had been previously.

C43 *Plate*, c. 1800
Diameter: 8½ inches
Loan: Brooklyn Museum, gift of Mrs. William Sterling Peters

The heavily patterned enamel and gilt border on this plate is typical of the turn of the nineteenth century. A shield on an ermine mantling bears the initials "S.J."

Samuel Jackson, whose family was among the first members of the Society of Friends to settle on Long Island, was born in Jerusalem, Long Island, and owned a substantial estate in Brooklyn Heights in the late eighteenth century. His home was famous for its ornamental gardens and many people visited to see them. He was a

successful businessman, who was reputed to make more money by staying home in Brooklyn and directing his affairs from there than he could have by working in New York City.

C44 *Pair of Urns*, c. 1800
Height: 15 inches
Loan: Albany Institute of History and Art (1940.713.1 A–D)

Pistol-handle urns have a long history, back to designs by Stefano della Bella in the late sixteenth century. The immediate forerunners of those produced in China after 1790 were made by Wedgwood. The decoration over molded leaves and a husk chain and above a marbled base is predominantly in blue and orange. It highlights raised oval medallions on either side, one with a temple among trees painted in ochre, the other with the scene of "L'Urne Mysterieuse."

This latter medallion, after a print published originally in France in 1793, shows the white profiles of Louis XVI and Marie Antoinette on either side of the urns, as well as images of the Dauphin and Madame Royale. The design had a strong sentimental appeal to those Royalists who fled the Terror during the French Revolution, yet few pieces have survived with proven histories in the families of those that escaped.

This pair, therefore, is quite remarkable, for it was once owned by Mme. Hazen, *née* Charlotte de la Saussaye, of Montreal, Canada, who married General Moses Hazen in 1770. In her will, Mme. Hazen named Lieutenant Governor John Tayler of New York as her executor and bequeathed the two urns to his daughter, Margaret Vernor Tayler (1773–1860), later Mrs. Charles De Kay Cooper of Albany.

Subsequent owners included Mrs. Cooper's daughter, Elizabeth (1807–1867), who married Benjamin Nott of Albany; Susan Benedict Nott (1843–1919), later Mrs. A. Douw Lansing of Albany; and the latter's children, Gertrude Lansing, Anna Lansing, and Cooper Nott Lansing. Together, the children gave the urns in memory of their parents to the Albany Institute of History and Art in 1927.

A very similar pair of urns, once the property of Joseph Bonaparte of Bordentown, New Jersey, is at the Henry Francis du Pont Winterthur Museum.

c45 *Pistol-Handle Urn*, c. 1800

Height: 17 inches
Loan: Bernard and S. Dean Levy, Inc., New York City
Photograph: Courtesy of Bernard and S. Dean Levy, Inc., New York City

This urn, derived originally from a late sixteenth-century Italian design, but more immediately after Wedgwood, resembles a number of others in this exhibition in its form and decoration (cat. c44 and c46). The enamels are predominantly blue with orange and gold; the base is marbled. One side bears the crest of Duane, "a demi wolf rampant," although in England the Duane crest is recorded as "a wolf's head erased." On the other side, an oval with the initials "M.A.L.D." appears within a mantle.

This urn was made for James Duane, the first post-Revolutionary mayor of New York. The initials are those of his wife, Mary Alexander Livingston Duane. James Duane, an attorney, was a delegate to the first Continental Congress. He served as mayor of New York from 1784 to 1789, when Richard Varick succeeded him (cat. B19). In 1789 he became a judge of the United States District Court. John Trumbull completed a portrait of Duane in 1800.

c46 *Pair of Urns*, c. 1800

Height: 23 ½ inches
Collection of The New-York Historical Society, gift of the Beekman Family Association (1965.4A–D)

This large pair of pistol-handle urns with covers follows a Wedgwood pattern. It is enameled in blue and orange with marbled base. This pair has oval medallions painted in ochre with realistic country scenes based on engravings.

A note found at the time of the bequest contained the following information:

c46

c45

These vases came from the old homestead of my grandfather, Benj. Hoppin probably brought from China ... by my uncle Col. Carrington (?)

The connection with the Beekman Family Association is probably explained by the marriage of Catherine Beekman (1841–1923), the daughter of James W. Beekman (1815–1877), to William W. Hoppin.

c47

c48

C47 *Part of Tea Service*, c. 1800
Height of caddy: 6 inches, including cover
Loan: Sleepy Hollow Restorations, Tarrytown, New York (v.c. 58.180 and v.c. 58.160–163)

The varied decoration—including a husk chain, blue enamel band and gilding, and the initials "A.S." in a roundel surrounded by an eight-point gilt star—is an example of one of the more elaborate styles of tea services at that date. Such decoration was much more popular in the American than in the European market.

"A.S." stands for Anne Stevenson, the second wife of Pierre Van Cortlandt (1762–1848), whom he married in 1813 and who died only eight years later. The service was probably made before her marriage, for her initials would otherwise have been different, but how long before is not certain.

Reference: See Joseph T. Butler, *Sleepy Hollow Restorations: A Cross Section of the Collections* (Tarrytown: Sleepy Hollow Restorations Collections, 1983), 97.

C48 *Part of Tea Service*, c. 1800
Width of teapot including handle: 9½ inches
Loan: Anonymous
Photograph: Clem Fiori

This tea service of an unusual style has a blue enameled rim with gilding and engrailed edging in gold. Each piece has an eight-point star. The roundel in the center of each star is empty. Each piece also bears a letter "D" in script and a talbot crest for Drew, although this is not recorded in reference books. The teapot has a domed cover, unusual for this period, which may be from another piece of the service.

The service was made for Lydia Watkins Drew, who had married Captain James Drew in 1792. He was drowned when his ship foundered in a storm off Cape May, New Jersey, in 1795 and is buried in St. Peter's Church, Lewes, Delaware. His widow later married James Beekman and lived in Princeton. Lydia Watkins Drew's sister, Elizabeth, married Robert Henry Dunkin (see cat. B27 for their armorial service).

C49 *Teabowl and Saucer*, c. 1800
Diameter of saucer: 5½ inches
Loan: Abigail Adams Smith Museum, New York City

The service of which this bowl and saucer are a part is one of the most elegant of the period. Each piece has a plain gold and blue enamel rim and a graceful cypher, "E.T."

Labels on the service record that it was made for E. Tapole. It has been in the Smith family since Mrs. Abigail Adams Smith, daughter of President John Adams and sister of President John Quincy Adams, lived in the New York house on what is now 61st Street (cat. C36).

C49

C50 *Teabowl and Saucer*, c. 1800
Diameter of teabowl: 3½ inches
Diameter of saucer: 5½ inches
Loan: Sleepy Hollow Restorations, Tarrytown, New York (v.c. 149 and v.c. 150)

These pieces from Van Cortlandt Manor are of a standard decoration. A blue enamel band with stars encircles a tightly hatched gold band. Sprays of flowers in gold and rust decorate the center.

C50

C51 *Small Bowl*, c. 1800
Diameter: 5⅜ inches
Loan: Sleepy Hollow Restorations, Tarrytown, New York (v.c. 58.200)

This piece may have been the slop bowl of a tea service, or it may have served some other, unidentified purpose. Its bands of orange and lavender and the sprays of *famille rose* flowers are typical of the late eighteenth century, but the outer rim design probably betrays a date of 1800.

This piece has a long history at Van Cortlandt Manor. (Shown on p. 108.)

C52 *Punch Bowl*, c. 1800
Diameter: 11 inches
Loan: Diplomatic Reception Rooms, United States Department of State, gift of Mrs. George P. Morse

This bowl has an unusual border decoration of fruit and flowers between two gold bands. A most unusual eagle holds a trumpet and shield with anchor in its talons and a ribbon in its beak with the motto, "In God We Hope."

A tea service with this eagle and motto is at the Henry Francis du Pont Winterthur Museum and the same eagle is engraved on a Chinese clock in a private collection. Apart from these, this punch bowl, with the eagle painted three times, is one of only two other recorded examples (cat. C53).

The bowl was made for John Jay (1745–1829), the sixth son of Peter and Mary (Van Cortlandt) Jay of New York City. John Jay came to prominence as the secretary of the royal commission of 1773 which fixed the boundaries between New Jersey and New York. After serving as president of the Continental Congress, he became chief justice of New York in 1779. By 1780 he was minister plenipotentiary to Spain. In 1782 Benjamin Franklin summoned him to Paris to become joint negotiator for peace with Great Britain. Declining the post of ambassador to Great Britain, he received a congressional appointment in 1784 as secretary of foreign affairs, a post which he held until 1790, when he was nominated chief justice of the United States. In 1795 he was elected governor of New York for the first of two three-year terms. Late in 1800 he retired to his farm in Westchester County, where he lived out twenty-eight years of retirement.

It would be appropriate to guess that Jay received this bowl as a gift at the time of his retirement as governor of New York after a varied and remarkable career in public service. An earlier dinner service apears in this catalog (cat. a16).

c53 *Plate*, c. 1800
Diameter: 9¼ inches
Loan: Anonymous

This plate has an unusual border of gilt vine tendrils and leaves with grapes enameled in blue. An unusual eagle holding a trumpet and shield with anchor in its talons and a ribbon in its beak bearing the motto, "In God We Hope," appears in the center. The initials "M.S." are above the eagle within an oval of stars.

The other porcelain examples of this eagle are a service at the Henry Francis du Pont Winterthur Museum and the John Jay punch bowl (cat. c52). The initials have not been identified and there is no certain New York provenance.

c54 *Pair of Custard Cups with Covers*, c. 1800
Height: 3 inches
Loan: Peter Trowbridge Gill

Covered custard cups like these were essential to smart entertaining in the late eighteenth and early nineteenth centuries. They were also known as *pôts de crème* for their use with cream custards and syllabubs. Twelve to eighteen per porcelain tray would have been set out on a buffet table. They are painted with a gold vine pattern at the rim. The initials on the shield are "J.L.H." or "F.L.H." or just possibly "H.L.H."

The service was made for the Hemmingway family of New York, maternal ancestors of the Low family.

C51

C52

c55 *Basket Stand*, c. 1800
Length: 10⅞ inches
Collection of The New-York Historical Society, gift of Gouverneur Kemble (1923.52)

This oval platter has a reticulated or pierced rim of a typical Chinese pattern. It was used as a stand for a fruit basket, which was also reticulated. The decoration is a plain gold band at the rim and well and the initials "I.G." in script in the center.

This stand was made for Isaac Gouverneur (1749–1800), a New York City merchant. It may have been presented to him for his fiftieth birthday as part of a dessert service.

C53

c54

c55

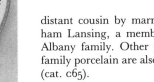

c57

c56 *Plate*, c. 1800

Diameter: 9⅞ inches
Loan: Historic Cherry Hill, Albany, New York (1705.4)

This plate has an elaborate red, blue, and gold border and a chain at the well. A roundel with a rural river scene in sepia is in the center. Mrs. Edward Rankin of Cherry Hill received the plate from her distant cousin by marriage, Mrs. Abraham Lansing, a member of a long-time Albany family. Other pieces of Lansing family porcelain are also in this exhibition (cat. c65).

c57 *Two Punch Bowls*, dated 1801

Diameters: 14½ inches and 13½ inches
Loans: Albany Institute of History and Art (1979.16) and Reeves Collection, Washington and Lee University (illustrated) (271)

Each of these plain bowls is decorated with a gilt rim and an American eagle with a sunburst in sepia. A shield on the eagle's chest bears the initials "K.V.R."

Kiliaen K. Van Rensselaer was the son of Colonel Kiliaen Van Rensselaer and his wife Ariantje (Schuyler) Van Rensselaer of Greenbush, a family mansion across the Hudson River from Albany. He was born on June 9, 1763, in the old mansion, now known as Fort Crailo, that had belonged to his ancestors for many years. After attending Yale University for two years, he became secretary to General Philip Schuyler. Later, he studied law and embarked upon a political career in Albany that led to his election to Congress in 1801. Possibly the date in the well of the bowl marks that milestone in his career. He married Margaritta Sanders, daughter of John and Deborah (Glen) Sanders of "Scotia," a mansion on the Mohawk River opposite Schenectady. Kiliaen died on June 18, 1845.

c58 *Tureen Lid*, c. 1805

Length: 9¾ inches
Loan: Historic Cherry Hill, Albany, New York (1704)

The only piece of the Van Rensselaer dinner service at Cherry Hill is this tureen lid. It illustrates a charming and possibly unique service. The broad band of border with flowers is edged with strips of gilding. Two roundels with brightly enameled butterflies are on the elaborate chain decoration.

This decoration may be unique. Pieces of the service grace a number of American museums. If the service were made for Cherry Hill, it would have been ordered by Maria Sanders Van Rensselaer (1749–1830), widow of Philip (d. 1798), or by her son, Philip, Jr. (1738–1827), but family tradition asserts it was made for Stephen Van Rensselaer III and then descended in the Turnbull family through Cornelia Paterson Van Rensselaer, second wife of Robert Turnbull, until the present century. In this case, the tureen lid would have been given to Cherry Hill at a later date. (Shown on p. 110.)

c59 *Miniature*, c. 1800

Height: 5 inches
Loan: Peter Trowbridge Gill

This miniature in an oval frame has the portrait of a middle-aged man wearing a black cravat. A merchant sailing ship is in the background. The painting is almost certainly by a Chinese artist.

The portrait is of John Broome, an active merchant in the China trade, who lived over his own store in Hanover Square in lower Manhattan. Immediately following the Revolution he was New York's principal tea merchant, importing two million pounds. He was chosen first alderman of New York in 1783 and lieutenant governor of the state in 1804. He gave his name to Broome Street.

c60 *Mug*, c. 1800

Height: 5⅜ inches
Collection of The New-York Historical Society, bequest of Mrs. J. Insley Blair (1952.121)

Simply potted, of cylindrical form with an entwined handle, this mug has a narrow husk and engrailed band at the rim. It is decorated in a stiff way with a three-masted merchantman lying at anchor. Its sails are furled, its ports are open, and it flies an American flag.

There is no way to know whether this particular mug was made for the New York market, but many similar ones certainly were. The ship on this piece appears to have been copied from a drawing of one off Whampoa Island, below Canton, but many were copied from illustrations of ships decorating cargo and mercantile documents.

c61 *Flagon with Cover*, c. 1805

Height: 11¼ inches
Collection of The New-York Historical Society, bequest of Mrs. J. Insley Blair (1952.116A and 1952.116B)

With an entwined double handle, a rising lip, and a cover with a dog of Fo, this flagon has a band of blue enamel with a gilt vine pattern. A continuous seascape, separated by an island, decorates the flagon. On one side of the piece a ship is sailing on a calm sea; on the other side, mountainous waves are battering a similar ship.

Flagons painted with the popular theme, "fair weather and foul," must have come to New York, although like exhibit c60, this

c58

c59

flagon has no New York provenance. The rim is certainly of a type popular in New York. Such flagons were often intended for cider or "small beer" (beer low in alcoholic content), but it is doubtful whether anything as original and charming as this was commonly used.

c62 *Chocolate Pot*, c. 1805

Height: 10¼ inches
Loan: Brooklyn Museum, gift of the Wyckoff family through Mrs. J. D. Lester (42.1212)

Whether this is a covered chocolate pot (as always known in the family) or a cider jug, the form is of the period 1800 to 1810. The broad band of flowers at the rim and on the lid is after English styles popular in the first decade of the century. The roundel on either side shows an avenue and a large house in sepia. The initials "F.W." in gold are on the front.

Captain John Ebbetts purchased the flagon in China and presented it to his neighbor, Folkert Wyckoff (1778–1814) of New

c60

c61

York. It is not known whether the scene is of the Wyckoff home, but the view is not a common one on porcelain.

Reference: For similar vessels with different decorations and themes, see Jean McClure Mudge, *Chinese Export Porcelain for the American Trade* (Newark: University of Delaware, 1962), 172 ff.

c63 *Pieces from a Dinner and Coffee Service*, c. 1804

Length of platter: 13¼ inches
Height of coffee pot: 9⅜ inches
Loans: Plate, *pôt de crème*, and coffee pot, Albany Institute of History and Art (x1940. 700.627, x1940.700.6(2)A–B, and 1971.8.1 A–B); platter (illustrated), Collection of Marjorie Van Schaick Emerson
Photograph: M. W. Sexton, Peabody Museum of Salem

This service with floral decorations is well documented and provides a firm date. The decoration is sparse on the larger pieces, but well painted. The crest of Van Schaick and the initials "G.W.V.S." are finely done. The whole armorial of Van Schaick includes a shield with a bull's head between three arrows, one horizontal and two upright, and the motto "Amor Amicitia Regnent," but it is only known on pieces of silver.

Gerrit Wessels Van Schaick, son of Wessel Van Schaick and Maria Gerritsen and grandson of Anthony Sybrant Van Schaick and Anna Catherine Ten Broeck (cat. B14), was born in 1758 and died in 1816 in Lansingburgh, New York. From 1792 to 1815 he was cashier of the Bank of Albany and was prom-

inent in civic and business affairs. He never married.

Mr. Van Schaick was a descendant of Goosen Gerritsen Van Schaick, who came to New Netherland in 1637. The first Van Schaick was a magistrate and prominent citizen of Beverwyck.

Gerrit Wessels Van Schaick was a friend of John Jacob Astor, whom he also served as banker. It was through Astor, who founded the family fortune and whose ships regularly traded with China, that he obtained the set of porcelain that these four pieces represent. The accompanying letters give an excellent idea of their friendly business relationship.

c64 *Correspondence from John Jacob Astor to Gerrit Wessels Van Schaick*, 1804–1805

Loan: Gansevoort-Lansing Collection, Rare Books and Manuscripts Division, New York Public Library, Astor, Lenox, and Tilden Foundations

Surviving correspondence between owners and suppliers of armorial porcelain is very rare. In England, the best known concerns two services made for the Peers family in 1731 and two consignments for the Okeover

family in 1739 and 1743. The 1760 account books of the Morant family of Jamaica mention their service, and correspondence regarding the Sykes service ordered through the Swedish East India Company in the late 1750s has also survived.

Records have been better preserved in the United States. The earliest concerns the Cincinnati porcelain for George Washington (cat. B2 and B3). Thereafter, there are a number of examples; for instance, the order, invoice, and will of a Mrs. Fuller of Philadelphia, who ordered some china "of the most fashionable kind" in 1787 through Captain Thomas Truxton.

On both sides of the Atlantic there was always a link between captain, merchant, and customer, for often they were friends, business partners, or relations. One did not entrust an order for something as personal as armorial porcelain to a stranger. The easy tone of the correspondence from John Jacob Astor to Gerrit Wessels Van Schaick bears out their friendship. The letters are in the hand of a clerk, for Astor's own writing was very difficult to read. They are simply addressed, "G. W. Van Schaick, Esqr., Albany."

New York 20 April 1804

Dear Sir,
With this you'll please receive by Cap^n Storrer

c62

c63

two boxes of China Marked GWVS No. 1 & 2 which Contain your table Sett and which I hope will come safe to hand & please you.

I am Dear Sir your most Humble Servant
John Jacob Astor

New York 21 April 1804

Dear Sir,

I shipped yesterday on board Captn Storrer Two boxes China which came in my vessel from Canton for you. Captn Storrers Sloop Lay Close by the ship which induced me to ship them by him — I hope he will take good care of Them as he was chargd So to Do & that it will please you Chinia is higher in Canton than it was Last year which may be one reason why yours may cost more than you expect on the other sied you have particulars of cost & charges for which you may give me cridet in the Bank or other ways — when I See you it will Do as well to pay me then.

We have now 30000$ or upwards of your Bank notes in the Manhattan....
John Jacob Astor

New York 20th April 1804

Dr. G. W. Van Schaick Esqr.
   To John Jacob Astor

1 Sett Tea China 88 ps $40		
1 Do. Dining "169" .... $80.	120.	

————Charges————

Insurance 10 per Cent	12	
Commission at Canton 3 pCt .	3.60	
Interest of Money Yr. @ 7 pCt	8.40	
Duty 18 per Cent	21.60	45.60
	Dollars	165.60
JJA		7
		172.60

New York 5 May 1804

Dear Sir,

I have your esteemed favor of 25 ulto and am really sorry to find that the amount of your China was left out you'll find it on the other Side I feare you'll think it high the truth is that China came this yeare 25 to 20 [per cent?] higher than Last. I am happy to find that nothing but Some of the plates are broken. if you'll be so good as to send me one of them I will Send it to Canton & have Some made for you of the Same — I shall have 50 to 55000$ of your Bank notes say in all next

week and on or about the 15 It [instant] you'll receive them when you'll have it in your power to oblige me in a most particular manner.

We have this moment a report that the King of england is dead which is believed to be true. there is still a very grat presure among us Dollars are however not So Scars as they were whether the Demand from them is less or that So many have been brought from the Country I know not but I hope you have plenty of them in your Bank —

I am, Dear Sir, with very great Respect your most Humble Servant
John Jacob Astor

New York 21 March 1805

Dear Sir

I send you by the Sloop vanrensler Captn Dacks a Box containing the China you ordered. I had for gotten to send The pattern plate by him & have therefor send it by Captn Doty — I wish the China may be in good order & to your Satisfaction the amount of Cost, we will Setteld one of these Days — mean time I am
Dear Sir with due respect and offer of my services yours
John Jacob Astor

Dr. G. W. Van Schaick Esqr.
   Newyork, 21 march 1805
To John Jacob Astor

No. 101 — 1 Box china ware as follows_____

	m.c.		L m c
4 sauce Boats .....@	4.2	-	1.6.8.
4 do cups	7.5	-	3 - -
1 Coffee pot			$.8.2
2 Sugar cups	4.4	....	8.8
4 Fruit Baskets......	1.1.5	......	4.6
48 flat plates	3.9	....	18.7.6
4 pudding dishes.....	3.7	......	1.4.8
1 Punch Bowl.............		1.1	-
2 do. do		1.6.	-
1 dozen cups & saucers .	2.3	....	2.7.6.
6 pickle dishes	2.6	....	1.5.6
4 cake do	3.5	....	1.4. -
	Tales		39.6.4
Deduct for Breakage 2 plates			7.9
			38.8.5

@ 75 candarins per Dollar .... is	$51.80	
Insurance on do	4.7	
Commission in Canton ..	1.10	
Freight from Do	10. -	
Interest on money	3. -	
Duty here	11. -	29.20
		$81.00

N.B. There is one plate here, which shall be sent per first safe opportunity, in a few days.

c65 *Coffee Pot and Sugar Bowl,* c. 1805

Height of coffee pot: 9¾ inches
Height of sugar bowl: 5¾ inches
Loan: Albany Institute of History and Art
[x1940.700.3(9)ᴀʙ and x1940.700.3(10)ᴀʙ]

Each piece of this service bears the initials "J.L."; "J. A. Lansing" is written in faded ink on the label of one. This is the only clue for determining which John Lansing was the owner among the many who lived in Albany.

According to the system of patronymics that the Dutch used, as his middle name each son took his father's first name. At the start of the nineteenth century, there were several men named John A. Lansing in Albany. The most likely was John A. Lansing (1749–1825), the son of Abraham and Elizabeth (Cooper) Lansing. He married Elizabeth Fryer in 1776 and was a veteran of the American Revolution.

The Lansing family was of Dutch descent. They originally spelled their name "Lansingh." The immigrant ancestor, who is said to have come to New Netherland about 1640, was Gerrit Frederickse Lansingh from Hasselt in the province of Overijssel. With his wife, Elizabeth Hen-

c65

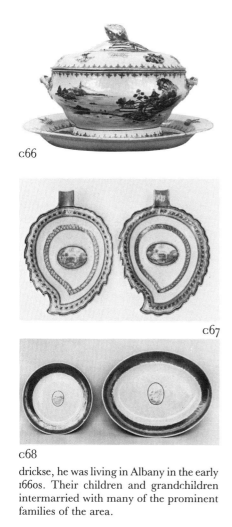

c66

c67

c68

drickse, he was living in Albany in the early 1660s. Their children and grandchildren intermarried with many of the prominent families of the area.

c66 *Tureen, Cover, and Stand; Platter, Tray, and Fourteen Soup Plates*, c. 1805

Diameter of tureen stand: 15½ inches
Loan: Tureen, cover, and stand (illustrated), New York Society of Colonial Dames; platter and plates, Collection of The New-York Historical Society, gifts of Iola Stetson Haverstick in memory of her mother, Iola Wise Stetson (1978.43 and 1978.44 A–N); tray, Collection of The New-York Historical Society (x.512)

This fine and very large service has a unique design, and is decorated in polychrome enamels with a realistic lakeside scene of a house in the foreground and a peninsula in the middle distance. This scene is within a spearhead border. On the rims are a number of Chinese deities and the initials "D.W.M.C." It has already been suggested that this design is derived from a Van Rensselaer service of which a piece is at Cherry Hill. The owner of this service knew the Van Rensselaers well (cat. A14).

The service bears the initials of DeWitt Clinton (1769–1828) and his wife, Maria (Franklin), whom he married in 1796. De-Witt Clinton was a giant in the political life of New York City and New York State in the first two decades of the nineteenth century. His grandfather, whose family was originally English, had come from Longford, Ireland, in 1729 and settled in Orange County. His father, James, was a major general during the Revolutionary War and his uncle George was the first governor of New York State. By the age of twenty-one, DeWitt, who had studied law and been admitted to the bar, was private secretary to his uncle, the governor. He held this position until his uncle's defeat in 1795. DeWitt was elected to the New York Assembly in 1797. By 1802 he was a United States senator. The following year he became mayor of New York, a position he held for all but two years until 1815. In 1812 he was a candidate for president, but he was defeated by the incumbent, James Madison. In 1817 he became governor of New York.

In the late 1810s, Clinton turned his attention to developing a canal between the Hudson River and the Great Lakes. He was governor in 1825 when the Erie Canal opened. Clinton died suddenly at his residence in Albany in 1828. He had married for a second time after Maria's death in 1818 and left seven children.

c67 *Part of a Service*, c. 1805

Loans: Pair of vegetable tureens and liners and pair of leaf-shaped dishes (illustrated), Peter Trowbridge Gill; pair of large platters, collection of Erving and Joyce Wolf; platter, Mr. and Mrs. George Kaufman

This service has a band of coral, sepia, and a gold wave pattern with some blue enamel at the rim. Its dual vignettes of a large house, avenue, and trees are in sepia. Except for the blue enameling, the style duplicates a service made about 1802 for Baroness Abercromby. The initials above the house are "J.S." or possibly "T.S."

The service was made for the Stagg family of Staten Island, although it is not clear for which member. John and Thomas Stagg were builders. John Stagg submitted bills to the New York City Council in 1771 for a new market and in 1781 for new powder houses. Trinity Church paid Thomas Stagg for improvements in 1786. In the city directory of 1810, a Thomas Stagg, Jr., is shown as a merchant at 345 Broadway. It is not clear whether the mansion on the service was built by the Stagg family or whether they resided in it.

c68 *Oval Platter*, c. 1806

Length: 12 inches
Loan: Mr. William Banks

This platter belongs to a varied dinner service. It comprises at least three types of tureens, a variety of dishes and plates, fruit baskets and stands, and a tea service. All are decorated with deep coral bands at the rim. In the center, an oval medallion has a white swan painted on an expanse of water.

It may be more than coincidence that the Pell arms have a pelican in both the crest and shield, and an heraldic pelican is painted as a swan. The service's naturalistic treatment is in keeping with sentiment in New York at the time.

Members of the Pell family, descended from John Pell of Pelham, were prominent merchants in New York City after the Revolution. One traded in imported timber, while another developed new varieties of apples on his fruit farm at Esopus. Alfred Pell married the daughter of Colonel James Duane, the first post-Revolutionary mayor of New York. This service was made for Mary Cornell Pell as a gift from her parents when she married Robert MacComb in 1806.

Service sold: Sotheby Parke Bernet, January 29, 1976, lot 88, *et seq.*

c69 *Oval Platter,* c. 1800–1810
Length: 15 inches
Width: 12 inches
Loan: Reeves Collection, Washington and
Lee University

This platter is decorated plainly with a
broad band of purple at the rim. In the
center there is an armorial consisting of a
shield and crest. The arms are the same as
those on an early nineteenth-century bookplate of the Lloyd family of Long Island.

Henry Lloyd II of Lloyd's Neck was a
Tory. He left for England at the time of the
Revolution and lived there for many years.
His estates were confiscated and sold in
1784 to his nephew, John Lloyd II, for
£2,900. The estate then consisted of a
700-acre farm and the Lloyd mansion. John
Lloyd continued to correspond with his
uncle Henry in London, but died young in
1792, leaving a substantial estate worth
£7,745. By 1809, when the heirs of John
Lloyd II had finally inherited the estate, it
was 1,800 acres in extent. The head of the
family in America was his son, John Nelson
Lloyd, educated at Yale and established in
New York as a merchant. It may have been
John Nelson Lloyd who ordered this service.

The Reeves Collection at Washington
and Lee University also contains a hot water plate from this service.

c70 *Platter,* c. 1810–1820
Length: 17½ inches
Catalogued, but not exhibited

This dish is part of a service decorated in
coral, brown, black, and gold. The rim
has stylized neo-classical pineapples. Figures of dignitaries standing between sprays
of foliage surround a central floral roundel.
The service is reputed to have belonged to
the Minor family of New York, although
there must have been more than one service, for some known pieces have crests.

Reference: For a service with a crest, see
Elinor Gordon, ed., *Chinese Export Porcelain*
(New York: Universe Books, 1975), color
plate 3.

c69

c70

c71 *Punch Bowl,* 1812
Diameter: 21½ inches
Loan: Punch bowl, City of New York (on
permanent loan to The Metropolitan Mu-
seum of Art, New York City); engraving,
Collection of The New-York Historical
Society

This remarkable punch bowl has a capacity of eight gallons. On the inside it is decorated after a colored engraving of New
York harbor by Samuel Seymour, published
by William Birch of Pennsylvania in 1802.
The inscription, "Drink deep. You will
preserve the City and encourage Canals,"
is inside the rim.

On the outside of the bowl, painted predominantly in sepia and gold, is the only
known example of the arms of the City of
New York on Chinese porcelain. An inscription on the outside of the rim reads
"Presented by General Jacob Morton, to
the Corporation of the City of New York,
July 4th, 1812." On the footrim is the further
inscription, "This bowl was made by Syng-
chong in Canton Fungmanhe Pinxit."

Brigadier General Jacob Morton played
an important part in the development of
New York City between 1790 and 1820. In

C71 INSIDE

C71 OUTSIDE

C71 VIEW OF NEW YORK

1793 he was involved in the plans to build the New York Society Library. A decade later in 1803 he sat on the commission for the building of the new city hall. He commanded the First Brigade of City Artillery in 1805 and became a member of the State Board for Fortifications. His troops were specially reviewed by Governor Tompkins and General Stevens in 1811. He was still active in planning as late as 1831.

C72 *Plate*, c. 1812
Diameter: 9⅞ inches
Loan: The Dietrich Brothers Americana Corporation, Philadelphia
On loan to: The Diplomatic Reception Rooms, United States Department of State
Photograph: Will. Brown, Philadelphia, Pennsylvania

This is from an elaborate service with three separate decorative motifs. The outer rim has a coral and sepia leaf chain, as on services of about 1800; inside is a ribbon and flower festoon band in sepia, also resembling services of about 1800. In the center there is a rather crudely painted display of military implements, with an eagle resting on a cannon. This last design was probably created during the War of 1812. The service has no certain date. If the rim design is to be taken as a guide, it should be much closer to 1800.

The service was owned by Sylvanus Thayer (1785–1872), a military engineer and educator. Thayer was sent to Europe in 1815 to study military schools. On his return, he was appointed superintendent of the United States Military Academy at West Point.

Thayer found the Academy in a chaotic condition, but by the time he was relieved of command, at his own request, in 1833, it was an efficient and disciplined organization. Thayer did not retire from the army until 1863. Afterward, he founded the Thayer School of Engineering at Dartmouth College. (Shown on p. 116.)

C73 *Mug*, c. 1812
Height: 6 inches
Collection of The New-York Historical Society, bequest of Mrs. J. Insley Blair (1952.124)

This plain cylindrical mug with an entwined handle has a rim design of vine leaves. It is painted with the military eagle illustrated on the previous exhibit. At least two more designs with this eagle are known. There is no New York provenance. It is not known whether there is a common link between the owners of porcelain decorated this way. (Shown on p. 116.)

C74 *Sauce Tureen and Two Covered Cups*, c. 1812
Length of sauce tureen: 7½ inches
Loan: Cooper-Hewitt Museum, The Smithsonian Institution's National Museum of Design, bequest of Mrs. John Inness Kane (1926.22.145)
Photograph: Scott Hyde

This sauce tureen and two covered cups in the same collection belong to a large service decorated simply with a wide band of gold at the rim encompassing two foliate bands. An oval medallion in the center bears the initials "P.S.S."

The initials are of the Schermerhorn family, which descended from Jacob Schermerhorn. Jacob came from Holland on the ship *Van Rensselaerwyck* in 1636 and became one of the most prosperous traders in Beverwyck (Albany). A descendant, Simon, carried the news of the Schenectady massacre in 1690. Peter Schermerhorn, of a later generation, married Elizabeth Bussing; their daughter, Caroline, married William Astor. The family was related to the Beekmans, the Ten Eycks, and other prominent Dutch families. This service was made for another Peter, who married Sarah Jones in 1812. The service was almost certainly made at that time. (Shown on p. 116.)

C72

C73

C74

c75 *Meat Carving Platter and Mazzarine*, c. 1820
Length: 19¼ inches
Loan: Collection of Erving and Joyce Wolf

This deep dish with veining and a mazzarine, or strainer, is decorated in the "Fitzhugh" style in finely penciled sepia. It should be compared with the Manigault service, made for a Charleston family, and the Goldsborough service, made with armorials for a Baltimore family. This service has the simple letter "H" for the Hone family. All three services are of the same quality, and are from about 1820.

This service was probably made for John Hone, born in 1764, the elder brother of Philip Hone (1780–1851), whom he raised after their parents died of yellow fever. John Hone trained his brother, Philip, as an auctioneer. Their firm was so successful that in 1815 its net profits were $159,000. Philip retired in 1821, toured Europe, devoted time to his large art collection, and was mayor of New York in 1825, when Lafayette visited the city. He also opened the Erie Canal. He is best remembered today for the daily diary that he kept from 1828 until five days before his death. In spite of his great wealth, he lost much of his estate in the Panic of 1837. After near bankruptcy, he was appointed naval officer of the port of New York by President Taylor.

John Hone II, Philip's nephew, married Marie Antoinette Kane in 1818. The service may have been made for this occasion. It was the property of their descendant, Mrs. Gouverneur Morris Phelps, until forty-seven pieces were sold at auction in 1976. Two Hone platters, loaned anonymously, are also in the exhibition.

c76 *Octagonal Platter*, c. 1800
Length: 12½ inches
Loan: Sleepy Hollow Restorations, Tarrytown, New York (v.c. 58.768)

This oblong octagonal platter, decorated in an underglaze blue, exhibits little artistry. The painting is realistic and has perspective, however, and the border pattern is complex and painstaking. It shows every sign of having been painted before the demands of mass production lowered quality. The painting was probably done in Ching-te Chen; the porcelain traveled to the merchants at Canton by way of Nanking, thus giving it this name. This platter belongs to a composite service of eighty-eight pieces long used at Van Cortlandt Manor.

c77 *Plate*, c. 1800–1810
Diameter: 9½ inches
Loan: Sleepy Hollow Restorations, Tarrytown, New York (v.c. 58.794)

This plate of a slightly shaped octagonal form is one of two matching pieces. It is an early example of Canton ware, painted in a style differing little from the so-called Nanking ware, which came from Ching-te Chen via Nanking. The finely painted lines and detail, both on the border and in the center, contrast with later plates. This plate was used at Van Cortlandt Manor as part of a composite service of eighty-eight pieces.

C75 PLATTER

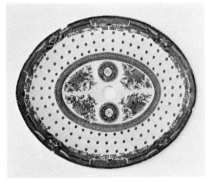

C75 MAZZARINE

c78 *Vegetable Dish and Cover*, c. 1800–1810
Length: 9⅝ inches
Height: 5½ inches
Loan: Sleepy Hollow Restorations, Tarrytown, New York (v.c. 63.17)

The fine painting of the pagoda and river scene in an underglaze blue and of diaper bands broken by panels of stylized flowers probably indicates a date not long after 1800. The artichoke finial is well-modeled and not flattened.

The tureen was a bequest to Van Cortlandt Manor from Miss Elizabeth Van Cortlandt Baldwin of Baltimore, Maryland. It had previously been in the Van Cortlandt family and was probably part of a dinner service.

c79 *Octagonal Platter*, c. 1810–1820
Length: 15½ inches
Loan: Sleepy Hollow Restorations, Tarrytown, New York (v.c. 58.770)

This oblong platter should be compared with exhibit c76. It has a border closely resembling the former, but the central river scene lacks the perspective and realism of the former. It is possible that this platter is the work of an inferior painter active at the same time as the artist responsible for c76, but this cataloguer believes that the piece was made a decade later. Although differing from the design on other pieces, it is one of a number of platters in a composite service at Van Cortlandt Manor.

c80 *Sugar Bowl and Cover*, c. 1820
Height: 5 inches
Loan: Sleepy Hollow Restorations, Tarrytown, New York (v.c. 58.712A–B)

This Canton ware sugar bowl with cover uses a shape which had been the accepted pattern for nearly fifty years. Handles on later examples like this one often "fold upwards" at the top. The pagoda and river scene in underglaze blue is better painted than in later Canton ware. The trellis pattern and edge pattern are recognizable as poorly imitative of the ware of the 1790s.

c76

c77

c79

This bowl belongs to a large composite service of eighty-eight pieces used at Van Cortlandt Manor. (Shown on p. 118.)

c81 *Vegetable Dish*, c. 1820–1830
Length: 9¾ inches
Loan: Sleepy Hollow Restorations, Tarrytown, New York (v.c. 58.775)

This Canton vegetable dish, or base of a vegetable tureen, is painted in a style that for this ware is refreshingly original. In the center, a sage and a lady sit on a promontory by a mountain lake, while a girl paddles by in a boat. Although the scene is quite different from other river landscapes on contemporary porcelain, the dish was used as part of a composite service of eighty-eight pieces at Van Cortlandt Manor. (Shown on p. 118.)

c78

c82 *Plate*, c. 1820–1840
Diameter: 9¾ inches
Loan: Sleepy Hollow Restorations, Tarrytown, New York (v.c. 58.777)

This Canton ware plate, one of a remaining group of fifteen, is poorly painted at the rim and may be compared in this respect with earlier piece above. This group was used as part of a composite service of eighty-eight pieces at Van Cortlandt Manor.

c83 *Tureen, Cover, and Stand*, c. 1830–1880
Length of stand: 13½ inches
Loan: Platter, Abigail Adams Smith Museum, New York City; advertisement, Bella C. Landauer Collection, The New-York Historical Society

This underglaze blue tureen and stand belong to a service used at the Abigail Adams Smith home on 61st Street, New York. The decoration, consisting of river scenes, trellised rim, and hoops, is perhaps the most popular scene of Chinese porcelain made for the American market. The service is all of the same, or very similar, pattern, but was probably bought over a number of years.

Evidence at various homes in New York State suggest that this pattern of Canton ware was being painted by about 1830. The pattern was still popular in 1880. The advertisement of Jones, McDuffee, and Stratton of Boston illustrates an almost identical tureen and stand in 1882.

c84 *Platter*, c. 1830–1880
Length: 12½ inches
Loan: Mrs. Florence Clark Frank

This Canton platter from a service (cat. c85) is painted in underglaze blue. The river scene at the center was popular for about fifty years. In 1886 the platter belonged to Salter Storrs Clark when he photographed his wife's inheritance. Mrs. Clark was the daughter of James Goddard, a New York merchant. James was the son of Eunice Rathbone Goddard, whose father, John Rathbone (1751–1843) of New York City, became active in the China trade late

c80

c81

c82

in the eighteenth century. In 1813 the firm John Rathbone and Son made a contribution of $20,000 to the government to support the war against England. According to family tradition, this China service came in a ship belonging to John Rathbone and Son.

c85 *Vegetable Tureen and Cover*, c. 1830–1880
Length: 9½ inches
Loan: Mrs. Florence Clark Frank

This rectangular vegetable tureen is from the same underglaze blue Canton service belonging to the Rathbone family as the platter also exhibited (cat. c84). The date could be anytime between 1830 and 1880, but is thought by the family to be earlier in this period.

c83

c84

c86

c85

c87

c86 *Octagonal Platter*, c. 1830–1880

Length: 14½ inches
Loan: Sleepy Hollow Restorations, Tarry-town, New York (v.c. 63.18)

This oblong platter, like a number of other pieces in this exhibition, is one example of the deterioration of design in this varied series of river scenes (cat. c83 to c85). The style is now naive. Clearly it is the work of Canton decorators, which accounts for much of the simplification of design both on the border and in the center. A number of similar pieces, including a milk jug of the same quality and border (v.c. 58.711), are at Van Cortlandt Manor.

c87 *Covered Custard Cup*, c. 1830–1880

Height: 3 inches
Loan: Sleepy Hollow Restorations, Tar-rytown, New York (v.c. 58. 714)

The form of these covered custard cups, established in France in the 1760s and soon copied in China, remained the same for over a century. The strawberry finial be-came "squashed" after the 1820s. Store ad-vertisements in the 1880s indicate that the underglaze blue decoration with pagodas, streams, and boats; Canton wash; and shaded rim patterns was still in use.

This cup is one of six in a set comprising eighty-eight pieces used at Van Cortlandt Manor and returned there from the collec-tion of Mrs. Robert P. Browne of Garden City.

Reference: Joseph T. Butler, *Sleepy Hollow Restorations: A Cross Section of the Collections* (Tarrytown: Sleepy Hollow Restorations, 1983), 97.

c88 *Small Mug*, c. 1830–1880

Height: 4½ inches
Loan: Sleepy Hollow Restorations, Tarry-town, New York (v.c. 58.77)

The underglaze blue painting in Canton style on this mug is particularly sketchy and irregular, and may well date from the later part of the nineteenth century. The stunted berry molding on the handle and the handle's upturned shape probably con-firm the date. Mugs were not necessarily bought with services, and variations be-tween their design and that of accompany-ing services is usual. This piece has a long history in the Van Cortlandt family. (Shown on p. 120.)

c88

c89

c90

c89 *"Blue China Dinner Sett,"* c. 1840–1850

Length of platter: 14⅝ inches
Loan: Historic Cherry Hill, Albany, New York (platter, 970; hot water plate, 143.2; sugar bowl and cover, 152A–B; milk pitcher, 182)

This variety of underglaze blue ware with river scenes and pagodas was made between the 1830s and 1880s (cat. c83, *et seq.*). Solomon Van Rensselaer's inventory of 1852 mentions "1 blue China Dinner Sett" and "1 blue China Tea Sett." The pieces exhibited here are almost certainly from these sets. Careful examination of the designs on various pieces shows that they were not all of exactly the same pattern. It was usual to buy replacement pieces as some were broken.

c90 *Teabowl and Saucer,* c. 1860–1880

Diameter of saucer: 6 inches
Loan: Sleepy Hollow Restorations, Tarrytown, New York (v.c. 58.749 and v.c. 58.755)

Decorated in a sketchy fashion in an underglaze blue, this bowl and saucer exhibit every sign of having been made with price in mind rather than quality. This type of Canton ware was painted very rapidly. The river and pagoda scene is much debased from work done earlier in the century. The bowl and saucer are one of six such sets in a composite service of eighty-eight pieces used at Van Cortlandt Manor. (Not illustrated.)

c91 *Oval Platter,* c. 1837

Length: 18 inches
Loan: Diplomatic Reception Rooms, United States Department of State, gift of Mr. and Mrs. Henry S. McNeil
Photograph: Diplomatic Reception Rooms, United States Department of State

This platter is heavily potted and decorated over the whole surface with small sprays of flowers. A continuous band of flower sprays is at the rim. This type of decoration is similar to a water bottle commemorating Queen Victoria's accession, dated 1837, and another with an eagle holding the yellow flag of China and the Stars and Stripes, displayed beneath a sunburst, at the Henry Francis du Pont Winterthur Museum.

The sixtieth anniversary of the surrender of General Burgoyne to General Gates at Saratoga was commemorated in 1837 and the ribbon in the mouth of the eagle reads "The Surrender of Burgoyne." The American victory at Saratoga encouraged the French entry into the Revolutionary War. The scene is sketchily copied from John Trumbull's painting, which is now at Yale University, but the Chinese artist has omitted Burgoyne's sword and shown him shaking hands with Gates. The cannon and crowd of officers in the Trumbull painting is missing here, but the American flag on the tent is present. Burgoyne's surrender was one of the most important moments of the war, and a natural choice as the only

c91

Revolutionary event commemorated on Chinese porcelain of this period.

Reference: David Howard and John Ayers, *China for the West* (London and New York: Sotheby Parke Bernet, 1978), 259; Arlene M. Palmer, *A Winterthur Guide to Chinese Export Porcelain* (New York: Crown, 1976), 140.

c92 *Portrait of Mrs. Caroline Hyde Butler Laing*, c. 1869–1870
Dimensions: 28¼ inches by 23½ inches
Medium: Oil on canvas
Loan: Mrs. Joseph Ashby Burton

This portrait of Mrs. Caroline Hyde Butler Laing (1804–1892) was painted in Rome in 1869 or 1870 by her son-in-law, T. Buchanan Read. Mrs. Laing was born in Oxford, New York, the daughter of Thomas and Sarah Denison Butler. She married Edward Butler in 1822. In 1836, concerned that she was developing consumption, she sailed to China with her husband on the ship *Roman*. The diary of her voyage is quoted in some length in Dr. Conrad Wright's introductory essay to this catalogue. She returned with a number of pieces of Chinese porcelain and other ware which are also exhibited here.

Edward Butler died in 1849. In 1851 Caroline married Hugh Laing; he died in 1869. She was the author of six books and numerous magazine articles, both fiction and travel pieces. Her diary's colorful tone and detailed descriptions ensure her a special place in the history of the American China trade.

c93 *Diary*, c. 1836–1837
Loan: Mrs. Thomas E. Ward, New York City

This is the diary kept by Mrs. Caroline Butler (1804–1892), wife of Edward Butler, during her voyages from New York to Canton and home, October 11, 1836–July 9, 1837. Mrs. Butler had sailed in hopes of curing her consumption; her long life is a testament to the efficacy of the treatment. The diary which she wrote and illustrated is quoted at some length by Dr. Conrad Wright in the introductory essay to this catalogue. It is a remarkable, readable, and historically interesting document.

c92

c93

c94 *Silk Apron*, c. 1837
Length: 31 inches
Loan: Mrs. Thomas E. Ward, New York City

Although cargo manifests show that considerable quantities of textiles were imported in crates and bales into the United States, especially before the mid 1820s, comparatively little has survived. The cloth was used for curtains, covers, shades, and clothing, and has worn out or fallen apart through up to two centuries of exposure to light. This apron of navy blue Chinese silk decorated with white floral borders, still in excellent condition, is an exception. Caroline Butler brought it home on the ship *Roman* in 1837.

c94

c95

c96

c97

c95 *Miniature Ivory Whatnot*, c. 1837
Height: 3½ inches
Width: 1½ inches
Loan: Mrs. Joseph Ashby Burton

This remarkable miniature, which seems to have had no functional purpose, was probably a toy or a novelty. The "whatnot," or shelved stand with turned pillars at each corner, copies a favorite mid nineteenth-century piece of furniture made for holding and displaying smaller decorative objects. In this case, the shelves contain miniature goblets, wine glasses, vases, covered sugar bowls, candlesticks, and a variety of other pieces. The intriguing objects in the center of the two lower shelves are unidentified.

This exhibit coincides with a vogue for miniature silver. Mrs. Butler almost certainly brought it back from China. (Shown on p. 121.)

c96 *Silk Winders and Needle Holder*, c. 1837
Loan: Mrs. Joseph Ashby Burton

Lacquer ware boxes from China delighted both the American and the European public in the nineteenth century. The boxes served a wide range of functions. There were caddies with pewter tea cannisters (cat. c103 and c104), game boxes (cat. c111),

work boxes, and many more varieties. These reels and silk winders came from a lacquer ware work box, probably from about 1837. The ivory needle case was probably in the same box. They belonged to Caroline Butler, who returned from China in 1837.

Reference: For a sense of the wide variety of lacquer ware objects imported from China, see Carl L. Crossman, *The China Trade: Export Paintings, Furniture, Silver & Other Objects* (Princeton: Pyne Press, 1972), 168–187. Other interesting pieces appear in Roderic H. Blackburn, *Cherry Hill: The History and Collections of a Van Rensselaer Family* (Albany: Historic Cherry Hill, 1976), 149.

c97 *Pair of Rose Canton Vases*, c. 1837
Height: 18 inches
Loan: Mrs. Thomas E. Ward, New York City

These Canton *famille rose* vases are decorated with tight floral scroll work. Rectangular panels of figures and flowers form three rows. The handles and other raised decoration at the neck take the form of stylized dragons. Caroline Butler brought the vases back from China in 1837 on the ship *Roman*. They are still in possession of the family.

Reference: John Quentin Feller, *The Canton* Famille Rose *Porcelains* (Salem: Peabody Museum, 1983).

c97a *Gaming Counters in Box,* c. 1840
Width of box: 2½ inches
Loan: Anonymous

From before 1720 until at least 1870, sets of mother of pearl counters were made for use with various card games. In the eighteenth century, many of the finest sets had armorials, which were frequently engraved with the same crests that appeared on armorial porcelain. Perhaps the earliest, from 1720, has the arms of Decker impaling Watkins. In the eighteenth century, counters were usually known as "fish" because they were often cut in that shape.

In the late eighteenth century and throughout the nineteenth century, counters used

c97a

for such games as Loo and Pope Joan were often sold in sets of lacquer boxes. Rather rarer were small personal sets, contained as in this case in a similarly carved Chinese box.

This one has the initial "K," probably for William Henry King, who purchased Kingscote at Rhode Island in 1863, or possibly for his nephew, David King, Jr. Both were partners of Russell & Co. in China (cat. C100A and C104A).

C98 *Punch Bowl*, c. 1840
Diameter: 16 inches
Loan: Abigail Adams Smith Museum, New York City

This large punch bowl, decorated with tightly packed floral decoration on gilding with reserves of Chinese figures and flowers, is of a style which gained popularity in the United States about 1840. It was still being made in a simplified form in the twentieth century. Today, the pattern is usually known as "Rose Medallion." This bowl has a history in the Pell family of New York, for whom a special dinner service was made in China in 1806 (cat. C68). The family gave it to the Abigail Adams Smith Museum.

C98

C99 *Saucer*, c. 1840
Diameter: 6 inches
Owned by: Henry Francis du Pont Winterthur Museum, Wilmington, Delaware (M75.130). Catalogued, but not exhibited.

This saucer, from a large dinner, coffee, and tea service, is decorated in orange with flowers and birds. A circular medallion with the initials "M.B.S." appears in the center. The service was made for Malcolm

Bull Smith of Smithtown, Long Island, and is one of two services which bear his initials in exactly this style. The other is of rose Canton design and was probably made in the 1860s.

C99

C99A *Portable Writing Desk*, c. 1813
Width: 19⅜ inches
Height: 7¼ inches
Collection of The New-York Historical Society, bequest of Mr. Herbert D. Halsey (1939.240)

This black lacquer folding box is painted in the Chinoiserie style with pagodas and figures and boats in a river landscape. The lid opens and the front turns down to reveal a felt writing surface which, when lifted, discloses two large compartments and three secret drawers. The gilt decoration should be compared carefully with lacquer ware from China in this exhibi-

tion. The naive painting and features of the figures reveal this as colonial work, perhaps from India or possibly the Philippines.

The box was once the property of John Cook Halsey of New York and is recorded as having returned with him from China in 1813. But the wide ranging trade of American merchants at this time makes other origins for this box quite acceptable.

C100 *Pair of Rosewood Chairs*, c. 1840
Height: 36 inches
Loan: China Trade Museum, Milton, Massachusetts

The backs of these rosewood chairs consist of a central roundel with a deer on rockwork beneath pine trees. The chairs are from the Shanghai residence of Russell & Co., a trading house with connections in New York and Boston. The firm originally traded in Canton, but moved to Shanghai after a fire burned the "factories" or count-

C99A

C100

inghouses on the Pearl River in 1856. It ceased to trade in the 1890s.

William C. Hunter, who was associated with Russell & Co. for many years, provided much of what we know about the tedium and excitement of the merchants' daily life in the second quarter of the nineteenth century through his book, *The Fan Kwai at Canton before Treaty Days, 1825–1844.*

C100A *Silk Fire Screen*, C. 1840
Height: 33 inches
Width: 21 inches
Loan: The collection of Kingscote, property of the Preservation Society of Newport County, Newport, Rhode Island

Fire screens became essential pieces of furniture in Europe in the early eighteenth century, when series of functional rooms replaced the great halls of earlier periods. The use of Chinese embroidered silks was unusual, except in smaller pole screens, until the mid nineteenth century; this is a good example of embroidered silk with brightly colored tropical birds on shrubs and rockwork. The frame and feet of lac-quered Chinese hardwood complete an unusually fine piece.

This was probably purchased by William Henry King, a merchant in China with Russell & Co., who had bought large quantities of Chinese export ware before he purchased in 1863 the house at Newport now called Kingscote. It is recorded that he brought his own furniture and paintings from his previous home when he moved there in 1864. This was almost certainly one of those pieces. It now stands below a portrait of the merchant, Houqua, in the library at Kingscote (cat. C101).

Reference: John A. Cherol, "Kingscote in Newport, Rhode Island," *The Magazine ANTIQUES* 118 (1980), 481.

C101 *Portrait of Houqua*, c. 1830–1840
Dimensions: 24½ inches by 18½ inches
Medium: Oil on canvas
Loan: Redwood Library, Newport, Rhode Island

Thirteen Chinese merchants paid their government large sums to participate in a monopoly trade with the Europeans and Americans. Of them, Houqua, the wealthiest and most successful, had developed a reputation of almost legendary proportions by the 1830s, when this portrait of him is dated. At his retirement in 1834, Houqua's wealth was estimated at $26 million; he died in 1843 at age 74.

George Chinnery was one of the most colorful British artists of the first half of the nineteenth century. He studied under Sir Joshua Reynolds and left England in 1802, never to return. After two decades in India, where he painted the principal officials and many Indian princes, he moved to Macao in 1825. He continued to paint in the Portuguese colony for the remaining twenty-seven years of his life. His influence on nineteenth-century Chinese export painting was considerable; today, the "school of Chinnery" encompasses a wide range of Chinese and European painting.

This portrait differs from another of Houqua owned by the Hongkong and Shanghai Banking Corporation, but there are many similarities.

Reference: For an illustration of the Hongkong and Shanghai Banking Corporation's portrait, see Robin Hutcheon, *Chinnery: The Man and the Legend* (Hongkong: South China Morning Post, Limited, 1975), 93.

C101A *Chinese Painting of Canton*, c. 1840
Dimensions: 35½ inches by 78½ inches
Loan: The Collection of Kingscote, property of the Preservation Society of Newport County, Newport, Rhode Island

Among the very large number of paintings of the river at Canton, this must rank as one of the most detailed and interesting. It was painted on canvas, c. 1840, by an unknown Chinese artist and shows a wide panorama of perhaps two miles of waterfront at Canton. The famed factories or Hongs are in the left center and the Folly Fort is in the right center. The river is not as wide as it appears in this picture, but this was the only way in which such a wide panoramic view could be painted.

William Henry King, a successful merchant with Russell & Co., brought this picture from China c. 1840. In 1864 he moved it with his other furniture to his newly acquired home, Kingscote, in Newport, Rhode Island. It now hangs there in the library,

C100A

C101

CIOIA

CIO2

facing a portrait of Houqua (cat. CIOI) and above a silk fire screen (cat. CIOOA).

Reference: John A. Cherol, "Kingscote in Newport, Rhode Island," *The Magazine ANTIQUES* 118 (1980), 481.

CIO2 *Painting, "A View of the Tea Process,"* c. 1800

Dimensions: 48¾ inches by 73 inches
Medium: Oil on canvas
Loan: Berry-Hill Galleries, New York

This painting by an unknown Chinese artist has been studied in detail and recorded in a number of publications. Starting in the far distance and working toward the foreground, it depicts in an idealized form the cultivation, preparation, and shipment of tea. The process is shown in ten stages: preparing the soil, watering the plants, gathering leaves, rolling them, crisping the tea by fire, packing it in chests, marking and binding the leaves, weighing them,

registering the weight, and shipping the chests on vessels bound for Canton.

This work may have been the source of a painting on the same subject by William Daniell, which was exhibited at the Royal Academy in London in 1810. Certainly, there are many similarities. The theme was already a favorite one, for a set of twenty-four blue and white porcelain dishes made for the Dutch market c. 1745 covers these and more detailed processes. The wallpaper at Saltram House in Devon, England, supplied in the late eighteenth century, also has this theme.

Following this painting and that by Daniell, smaller, utilitarian objects also took up the theme — for example, a remarkable pair of lacquer boxes with painted lids for tea (cat. CIO3). Thomas Allom, an English artist who generally worked from sketches, portrayed the same idea in his work, *The Chinese Empire Illustrated* (London, 1843), II, 34. Although Allom visited China after the First Opium War, it seems unlikely that his illustration is taken from

life. Toward the end of the nineteenth century, the advertisements of the Great American Tea Company used views which were inspired by this or similar paintings. These later views sometimes combined tea plantations in the background with the warehouses of Canton in the foreground.

The painting exhibited here, a clear and analytical view of the tea process, is in itself a remarkable example of Chinese export art. It has no New York provenance, having been discovered in England, but is illustrative of the main cargo of the China trade to New York — tea.

References: Thomas Sutton, *The Daniells: Artists and Travellers* (London: 1954); Kee Il Choi, *The China Trade: Romance and Reality* (Lincoln, Massachusetts: De Cordova Museum and Museum of the American China Trade, 1979).

CIO3 *Pair of Lacquer Boxes,* c. 1840

Height of boxes: 10⅜ inches
Dimensions of poster: 11⅛ inches by 14 inches
Loan: Pair of lacquer boxes, Mr. Reuben Getshow, Milwaukee; poster, Bella C. Landauer Collection, The New-York Historical Society

These remarkable lacquer boxes have gilding around the sides. On the top, one has a scene from a tea plantation; the other has a scene of a Chinese hong or warehouse on the Pearl River. Inside each box is a single pewter tea canister and cover. They do not have a New York provenance. These views may be compared with the painting, "A View of the Tea Process" (cat. CIO2), which illustrates in an idealized series the steps involved in the processing of tea. It may also be compared with an advertisement for the Great American Tea Company of New York, which documents most of the steps in processing tea, from growing on the bushes to the sorting, drying, packing, and selling. (Shown on p. 126; boxes not illustrated.)

Reference: Kee Il Choi, *The China Trade: Romance and Reality* (Lincoln, Massachusetts: De Cordova Museum and Museum of the American China Trade, 1979).

CI03A　*Lacquer Cigar Case*, c. 1840

Width: 14⅞ inches
Loan: The Collections of Chateau-sur-Mer, property of the Preservation Society of Newport County, Newport, Rhode Island

This hinged and lockable cigar case or humidor is of shallow rectangular shape and rests on four gilt claw feet. The lacquer is finely decorated with temples, gardens, and figures in rectangular panels. In the center of the lid is a cartouche with the initial "W." It was the property of William Shepard Wetmore of New York, who died in 1862. Wetmore was a prominent merchant in the China trade. He traded in China from 1833 to 1841 as a partner in Wetmore, Hoppin & Co. After his daughter married John Cryder, Wetmore was a principal of the renamed firm, Wetmore, Cryder & Co., which continued in business until 1874 (cat. CI08). The house he built at Newport, Rhode Island, for his retirement was enlarged by his son and named Chateau-sur-Mer.

CI04　*Lacquer and Mother of Pearl Tea Box*, c. 1885

Dimensions: 15½ inches by 14¼ inches by 19¼ inches
Collection of The New-York Historical Society (x.513)
Photograph: See color plate

This large rectangular box with cut corners is decorated with Chinese figures in landscapes of mother of pearl. The style of lacquer is known as *burgauté.* The box contains a single, rectangular canister of engraved pewter. The container has a circular lid and holds some remnants of tea. The original invoice is also enclosed. It reads:

> *Fishkill Landing 5 September 1856*
> *Miss Mary Verplank*
> *Bought of James E. Member*
> *(Grocer and Provision Dealer etc.)*
>
> $　c
> *1 Chest Black Tea #*$\frac{53}{14}$*/39 (lbs.) @ 45¢ 17 55*
>
> *Received Payment*
> *Jas E. Member*
> *per S. Underhill*

CI03A

CI04A

CI03

Throughout the last century, the better grades of such edibles as tea and ginger were often supplied in lacquer, pewter, or porcelain of a quality which is today considered very collectible. At the time, however, these containers were usually regarded as utilitarian.

CI04A　*Pewter Tea Caddy*, c. 1850

Diameter: 8¾ inches
Loan: The Collection of Kingscote, property of the Preservation Society of Newport County, Newport, Rhode Island

This six-lobed tea caddy or canister is made of pewter. Originally it was probably one of a pair in a lacquer box. It is decorated all over the surface with a fine stippled pattern of scrollwork, flowers, and insects. Sets of tea caddies like the one from which this comes allowed nineteenth-century hostesses to mix their own blends of tea from two or more containers.

Edward and William Henry King of New York and Newport were both in the China trade. From trading in China they eventually invested in real estate in New York and Newport, Rhode Island.

David King, Jr. (1839–1894), a nephew of William Henry King, may have brought this caddy from China. David entered the China trade at the age of seventeen as a clerk with A. A. Low & Bros. and sailed for Canton in 1858. He retired a very prosperous man in 1874 after sixteen years there, much of the time with Russell & Co. He remodeled the King family summer home in Newport and renamed the residence "Kingscote." King died in 1894 after an unsuccessful operation for appendicitis.

CI05　*Three Paintings*, c. 1850

Dimensions: 13¾ inches by 18½ inches (including frame)
Medium: Oil on canvas
Collection of The New-York Historical Society, gift of Miss Alice Temple Parkin, 1946 (1946.80–1946.82)

China trade paintings like these, which are oil on canvas, were sold either singly or in sets during the nineteenth century. The

CI05A

CI05B

CI04

CI06

CI05C

best must be counted as works of art; the worst are repetitive and inaccurate, for most were painted in studios from earlier works. This set is an excellent example, from about 1850, of such painting at its best, and illustrates:

a) Hong Kong Island, Victoria Peak, and the harbor, painted from Kowloon.

b) The foreign factories at Canton as they were shortly before their destruction by fire in 1856. The gardens had grown up on the parade ground before the factories, and the English-style church had been built by the early 1830s. The flags are of the United States, France, Great Britain, and Denmark. Such scenes were sometimes painted on punch bowls (cat. B15).

c) A rarer and more interesting view of the foreign factories looking at an angle along the buildings.

CI06 *Two Silver Forks*, c. 1810
Lengths: 7 inches and 8 inches
Loan: Brooklyn Museum, bequest of Samuel E. Haslett (21.331 and 21.332)

Forks like these, part of a complete service of silver flatware, were copied in China from European, usually English, originals. This pattern, "fiddle, thread, and shell," was perhaps the simplest yet most elegant of the half-dozen or more styles which employed a similar shell. The pieces were usually marked with pseudo London hallmarks; their purity was 880 parts per 1,000 or more.

These forks descended in the Haslett family of New York, and were bequeathed to the Brooklyn Museum by Samuel E. Haslett. The Museum of the Worshipful Company of Goldsmiths in London has a very similar fork marked "SS" for Sunshing.

Reference: H. A. Crosby Forbes, *et al.*, *Chinese Export Silver, 1785–1885* (Milton, Massachusetts: Museum of the American China Trade, 1975), 58.

CI07 *Silver Tureen*, c. 1843
Height: 10 inches
Length: 16¾ inches
Width: 10 inches
Loan: The Metropolitan Museum of Art; purchase, Robert G. Goelet Gift, 1967 (67.109A and 67.109B)

This tureen forms part of "perhaps the most impressive group of pieces of Chinese Export silver yet observed." It has an oval body on a splayed base. High relief, repoussé decoration, and chasing cover almost the entire surface with continuous scenes of oriental warriors in battle. The lid has a finial with a dragon's head, while the handles are formed as the entwined tails of two dragons. The silver has a Chinese "hallmark" drawn as a Lombardic "H." This mark corresponds to 1843 in the London series of date letters. The service is stamped with the mark of Hoaching.

Together with a number of other elaborate pieces, this was made for Abiel Abbot

C107

C108

C109

Low (1811–1893), founder of A. A. Low & Bros. of New York, a leading firm in the China trade. Abiel Low was affiliated with Russell & Co. in China between 1833 and 1840. This silver service remained in the family until the 1960s.

Reference: H. A. Crosby Forbes, *et al.*, *Chinese Export Silver, 1785–1885* (Milton, Massachusetts: Museum of the American China Trade, 1975), 109.

C108 *Silver Goblet*, c. 1856
Height: 6½ inches
Collection of The New-York Historical Society, gift of Henry Chauncey Cryder, son of William Wetmore Cryder (1947.16)

This standing cup with a bell-shaped body has applied decoration of military figures in action on foot and horseback. The scenes are said to be of an attack on Nanking. The gently splayed stem, which has applied work with leafy decoration, stands on a circular foot. A shield applied to the bowl bears the letter "C." This initial probably refers to John Cryder, a principal of the firm, Wetmore and Cryder. The firm ap-

parently ceased to trade temporarily in 1857; Cryder may have received the goblet at that time.

A series of companies connected with Cryder's family traded between 1833 and 1874. John Cryder married a daughter of William Wetmore, his partner, and had a son, William Wetmore Cryder. John Cryder left Canton around 1860, but his son remained as a director of the family firm.

C109 *Malacca Cane*, 1849
Length: 48 inches
Loan: China Trade Museum, Milton, Massachusetts

This gold-topped malacca cane is inscribed on its embossed knob, "Warren Delano, October 28th 1849." Warren Delano, who spent many years as a merchant in China, married Catherine, the daughter of Joseph Lyman, in the late 1840s. He died at Hyde Park, New York, in 1900. His youngest daughter, Sara, born in 1854, married James Roosevelt in 1880. She was the mother of Franklin Delano Roosevelt, thirty-second president of the United States, born in 1882 (cat. C126–C129).

C110 *Mother of Pearl Card Case in Brocade Case*, c. 1850

Length: 3¹¹⁄₁₆ inches
Loan: Anonymous

Mother of pearl objects made very popular gifts throughout the nineteenth century. They were both attractive and relatively inexpensive. This box is engraved with figures in a Chinese landscape within a floral border. The unidentified initials "I.H.D." are on a central oval. The same technique of engraving was employed on mother of pearl gaming counters. It was a feature of this ware that no two scenes were ever exactly the same.

This card case is still in its original brocade traveling case with the label, "W. I. Tenney. Jeweller, 251 Broadway. cor of Murray, New-York."

C110

C111 *Games Box*, c. 1850–1870

Dimensions: 16¾ inches by 10¾ inches by 5¼ inches
Loan: Anonymous

This rare games box is one of only two similar pieces recorded. It is of black lacquer. The name, Gardner Rand, and two sprays of bamboo are on the cover in gold. The box contains some twenty games, sets of blocks, puzzles, and rings, all made of ivory. The tassels are silk, as are the linings for the three trays on which the games are arrayed.

The box was made either for Gardner Rand, Sr. (d. 1867), or his son, Gardner Rand, Jr. (1832–1898). Both were businessmen and real estate dealers in Troy, New York. Neither had a known connection with China; the box may have been a gift or purchase. It is of the same quality as the pieces in the Catherine Van Rensselaer

Bonney Collection at Historic Cherry Hill (cat. C112). The China Trade Museum in Milton, Massachusetts, has a similar box. (Not illustrated.)

C112 *The Catherine Van Rensselaer Bonney Collection*

Cherry Hill: The History and Collections of a Van Rensselaer Family by Roderic H. Blackburn was published in 1976. The Van Rensselaers of Cherry Hill were descendants of the family at Greenbush and of Kiliaen Van Rensselaer (1585–1646), the Amsterdam pearl and diamond merchant who founded the family in America. It is worth quoting Blackburn's study of the Van Rensselaers at length, for Mrs. Catherine Van Rensselaer Bonney probably brought many pieces in this exhibition from China (C113–C120):

Catherine Visscher Van Rensselaer (1817–1890), daughter of Solomon and Arriet Van Rensselaer, was raised at Mt. Hope and Cherry Hill. She was trained as a teacher, a profession which she continued all her life. She and the Reverend Samuel Bonney were married in 1856 and shortly thereafter established a missionary school in China. Reverend Bonney died in Canton in 1864 but Mrs. Bonney continued her work in China until 1871 with a year's trip home in 1868. She acquired a considerable collection of useful and decorative Chinese products while in the Orient, which she shipped home to friends and relatives including part of which she kept for her own use. The illustrations reproduced here show the types of pieces which are believed to have been collected by Mrs. Bonney. Since no inventory of what she sent from China has been found, it is not possible to differentiate some items from what may have been purchased by the family here in America. The large quantities of similar types of porcelain, soapstone, lacquered and camphorwood pieces, and paintings of approximately the same style and date, however, make the supposition of one collection reasonable. One receipt for items purchased in 1869 by Mrs. Bonney is reprinted here.

Mrs. Van Rensselaer [possibly the wife of Dr. John Jeremias Van Rensselaer] gave me 25. = $112.90 Mexican.

	$	cts
Tea set – $54. + chamber set 57.00 +		
small articles 1.90	*= 112*	*90*
Mrs. Charles D. Thurn $65 in gold =		
$60.29		
2 large Vases 40.00 + Nest tables (4)		
20.29	*= 60*	*29*
Mrs. Elmendorf – Punchbowl & stand	*8*	*50*
Chess men 18.00 + Chess board 5.00		
(Margaretta)	*23*	*00*
Double washstand Crockery (HME)	*27*	*00*
24 small loegnes [sp?] plates	*5*	*00*
Box of tea 10 taels (HME)	*13*	*33*

The above account appears to represent Catherine Bonney's list of purchases and payments for various friends and relatives.

Because of its provenance, the whole collection at Cherry Hill is of the greatest interest and importance to the history of nineteenth-century Chinese porcelain, lacquer ware, and other decorative arts.

Reference: Roderic H. Blackburn, *Cherry Hill: The History and Collections of a Van Rensselaer Family* (Albany: Historic Cherry Hill, 1976), 143.

C113 *Soapstone Pagoda and Packing Case*, c. 1860

Height: 22¼ inches
Loan: Historic Cherry Hill, Albany, New York (1407A and 1407B)

Among the less studied minor decorative arts of China is the carving of soapstone, a steatite material, usually pale brown, and a "poor relation" of jade. The earliest finely carved pieces for the European market were of occidental, often religious, figures, c. 1700, and tea caddies in the early eighteenth century which were frequently stained and gilded.

In the nineteenth century, the souvenir market demanded spill vases, book ends, figures of monkeys, rockwork with birds, and occasionally more elaborate carvings like this pagoda. Each floor is made separately and fitted together. This example is remarkable for still being in its original wooden traveling case. It is one of six pagodas at Cherry Hill. Four are of this size. The softness of the stone allows elaborate surface carving. The same design on jade would involve a great deal of work because of its hardness. (Shown on p. 130.)

CII3

CII4

CII4 *Camphorwood Desk*, c. 1860
Height: 41¾ inches
Width: 38¼ inches
Loan: Historic Cherry Hill, Albany, New York (654)

This desk resembles European campaign chests. There are two full drawers and two half drawers (with sunken brass handles) standing on four turned feet. A separate upper desk section has side drawers with similar handles and a central sloping writing section which folds out in front of inner arched cubicles. The brass handles are either well copied or imported from Europe, where campaign chests and desks were in common use during the Peninsular War (before 1812) and in the Crimea (1854–1857). They were also used on various Indian campaigns. Camphorwood was used because it resisted the various beetles which might otherwise attack such furniture in the field.

This desk, one of two very similar ones owned by Mrs. Bonney and now at Cherry Hill, was a gift while she was in China.

CII5 *Camphorwood Chest*, c. 1860–1870
Dimensions: 29½ inches by 15½ inches by 11⅝ inches
Loan: Historic Cherry Hill, Albany, New York (657)

This plain, rectangular camphorwood carrying chest is one of two similar pieces at Historic Cherry Hill. It has iron handles and is bound with brass. Japanned sheet metal lines the inside. On the top, a label reads "M.V.R." for Margaretta Van Rens-

CII5

selaer. A label on the second chest at Historic Cherry Hill reads "Mrs. Bonney, Albany, N.Y." The chest with "M.V.R." is the smaller of the two. They were made in China, and were used for traveling both within China and on Mrs. Bonney's journey home. Margaretta Van Rensselaer was Mrs. Bonney's sister.

CII6 *Painted Wooden Birds*, c. 1870
Heights: from 3 inches to 6½ inches
Loan: Historic Cherry Hill, Albany, New York (269.1–5)

Among the more unusual objects at Historic Cherry Hill are these painted wooden birds. Their provenance has been lost, but they have been at Cherry Hill at least since the end of the nineteenth century. Most, but not all, are painted in a style which is unmistakably oriental. They were probably toys, brought back from China or Japan by Mrs. Bonney. Although only two are on exhibition, the illustration shows one of the shelves at Historic Cherry Hill on which the collection is displayed.

CII7 *Reverse Painting on Glass*, c. 1860
Height: 10 inches
Width: 7 inches
Loan: Historic Cherry Hill, Albany, New York (649)

The vogue for reverse painting on glass started in the first half of the eighteenth century, when fine English mirrors were decorated on the outer edge with Chinese designs. Later, a painting, now on Chinese glass, filled the whole frame. Frequently, the subjects were European or American colored engravings, or even paintings, as in the case of Gilbert Stuart's portrait of George Washington. The technique required the painting to be done in reverse order; thus a portrait started with the pupils of the eyes, followed by the whites, the eyebrows, and the rest of the face. Features tend to look a little hard in all but the very best examples.

By the second half of the nineteenth century, such paintings were frequently small and designed to satisfy an American demand for souvenirs of the China trade.

CII6

CII7

Beautiful Chinese girls, usually seated, half-length before heavy curtains, were most popular. As in this case, the frames were usually made in China after European styles of earlier decades.

CII8 *Washstand Set*, c. 1869
Diameter of punch bowl: 16⅛ inches
Loan: Historic Cherry Hill, Albany, New York (punch bowl, 339; vases, 1.1–2; nest of jars, 628.1A–B, 628.3A–B, 628.5A–B; nest of jars, 629.1A–B, 629.3A–B; mug, 621; mug, 626)

From 1865 on, there was a vogue for washstand sets in rich Canton *famille rose*. When President Ulysses S. Grant entered the White House in 1869 he received a similar dinner service of over 300 pieces (cat. CII21).

It is not certain that Mrs. Bonney purchased all these pieces in 1869. They do not appear in the 1852 inventory, however, and these or pieces of similar shapes do appear in photographs, c. 1880. An onion-shaped bottle and special washstand bowl with flared lip, which are not illustrated here, definitely appear in the photographs and are still at Historic Cherry Hill. A set comprising cylindrical boxes and covers, soap stands, and dishes was part of every properly equipped bedroom washstand at the time.

CII9 *Ivory Chess Set on Lacquer Board*, c. 1869
Dimensions of board: 19¼ inches by 19¼ inches
Loan: Historic Cherry Hill, Albany, New York (2191 and 2192.1–.32)

Fine lacquer ware, black on wood with intricate gold floral designs, was popular in the European market from the late seventeenth century until the middle of the nineteenth century and in the United States until perhaps the 1880s, when the quality seems to have deteriorated. Before 1750, this decoration was employed largely on cabinets and on panels which European master craftsmen used much like veneers, often on ormolu mounted furniture.

From the 1780s on, an increasing number of smaller objects, including games boxes,

CII8

work tables, work boxes, and nests of tables were made. Examples of most of these from the period 1850 to 1870 are at Historic Cherry Hill. This chess set and its board are particularly interesting, since both are mentioned in the 1869 receipt for items that Mrs. Bonney purchased (cat. CII2). Although these pieces are worth a great deal more today, their original prices — $18.00 for the ivory chess pieces and $5.00 for the lacquer board — are probably still in proportion to their modern values. Mrs. Bonney purchased them for her sister, Margaretta Van Rensselaer (1810–1880), who died unmarried.

Reference: For similar lacquer pieces, see Roderic H. Blackburn, *Cherry Hill: The History and Collections of a Van Rensselaer Family* (Albany: Historic Cherry Hill, 1976), 148–149.

CII9

CI20A

least three earlier styles of the period 1600 to 1720, is painted in a heavy way with little flair or artistry. Its form and quality are entirely consistent with pieces made after 1863 at Ching-te Chen, 500 miles north of Canton, shortly after the kilns there were rebuilt following the Taiping Rebellion. The piece was probably brought back to Cherry Hill about 1870, although it is not separately recorded.

CI20

CI20 *Punch Bowl*, c. 1870
Diameter: 14⅜ inches
Loan: Historic Cherry Hill, Albany, New York (183)

This bowl is very heavily potted. The underglaze blue design, while following at

CI20A *Nest of Lacquer Tables*, c. 1870
Height: 28½ inches (tallest table)
Loan: The Collection of Kingscote, property of the Preservation Society of Newport County, Newport, Rhode Island

It was very popular in the second half of the nineteenth century to have one or more sets of small tables in the drawing room. They were for serving tea and other occasional uses. When not in service, the smaller tables fitted inside the larger ones. This nest of Chinese lacquer has harp-shaped legs and gilt paw feet. It is typical of 1870. The tops are finely decorated in gilt scrollwork and each has the initials "D.K." The tables were made for David King, Jr., who was a merchant in China with Russell & Co. from 1858 until he retired with a considerable fortune to Newport, Rhode Island, at age thirty-six in 1874 (cat. CIO3A).

CI20B *Ivory Card Case*, c. 1870
Length: 4¼ inches
Loan: Anonymous

Carved ivory boxes were among many types of card cases favored in the second half of the nineteenth century. This is intricately carved with a continuous scene of figures in a landscape of terraces and pagodas. It was made for David King, Jr., who retired in 1874 after sixteen years in China with Russell & Co. (cat. CIO4A).

CI21 *Cup, Saucer, and Plate*, 1868
Diameter of plate: 9⅞ inches
Loans: Cup and saucer, Dr. John Quentin Feller; plate, Newark Museum, the gift of Mr. and Mrs. John S. Dietze (82.67)
Photograph: George Pugh. See color plate

Many porcelain services with initials and crests in a style now known as "Rose Medallion" were made between 1860 and 1880. The most popular design has four reserves on a tight scrollwork background of pink, gold, and green. Usually two of these designs around a central motif are of flowers and two are of figures.

In 1868, Captain Daniel Ammen, commander of the *Piscataqua*, returned from the Far East with two almost identical services. One, for his own use, bore the initial "A." The other, for General and Mrs. Ulysses S. Grant, had a Gothic cypher, "U.S.G." In early 1869 this service of over 300 pieces was delivered to the White House shortly after President Grant's inauguration.

Reference: For information on the exact dating of Rose Medallion, see John Quentin Feller, *The Canton Famille Rose Porcelains* (Salem: Peabody Museum, 1938), 24.

CI20B

CI2I

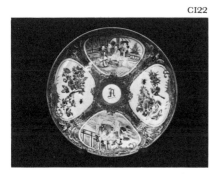

CI22

CI22 *Plate*, 1868
Diameter: 8 inches
Loan: Dr. John Quentin Feller
Photograph: Mark Sexton

This plate is exactly the same in design as the previous example made for President Grant. Captain Daniel Ammen (1819–1898), commander of the *Piscataqua*, bought this service of about 150 pieces for himself at the same time that he purchased President Grant's service. Ammen made arrangements with Olyphant and Co., an American firm based in Shanghai, to ship the two dinner services to New York in the fall of 1868. This service with the initial "A" he kept, while he delivered the other to the White House in early 1869.

Reference: John Quentin Feller, *The Canton* Famille Rose *Porcelain* (Salem: Peabody Museum, 1983), 24.

CI23

CI23 *Plate*, c. 1870
Diameter: 9¾ inches
Loan: Dr. John Quentin Feller

This plate is almost identical in decoration to the services made for President Grant and Captain Ammen (cat. CI2I and CI22). Ammen ordered only two services in 1868, but it is known that other naval officers purchased services at the same time. The cypher is "W.S." for William H. Seward (1801–1872). In 1838, Seward was elected governor of New York. During his four-year term he took an increasingly firm line against slavery. In 1848 he was elected to the United States Senate. By 1855, Seward embodied the antislavery sentiments of the north. Unsuccessful as a presidential candidate in 1860, he agreed in 1861 to serve as secretary of state under Abraham Lincoln. The most enduring accomplishment of his term in office was the purchase of Alaska, which he negotiated.

References: John Quentin Feller, *The Canton* Famille Rose *Porcelain* (Salem: Peabody Museum, 1983), 24–25; Feller, "The White House 'Rose Medallion': Daniel Ammen and the Ulysses S. Grant Porcelain," *American Neptune* 43 (1983), 177–185.

CI24 *Plate*, c. 1870
Diameter: 9⅞ inches
Loan: Dr. John Quentin Feller

The design of this plate is an interesting variation on a number of others in this exhibition (cat. CI2I, CI22, and CI23). The central medallion has a small aquatic scene and butterflies. A plain roundel with the initials "S.H.S." is between two of the panels. The service was made for Silas Horton Stringham (1797–1876), a naval officer born in Middletown, New York.

CI24

Stringham entered the service as a midshipman at the age of twelve in 1809 and took part in a number of actions during the War of 1812. During a career distinguished by several acts of great gallantry he commanded the U.S. Navy's Brazilian squadron in 1853 and its Mediterranean squadron in 1855. In March 1861 he was summoned to Washington. Although he was not stationed in time to contest for Fort Sumter, he commanded the Union fleet's Atlantic blockade and captured the forts at Hatteras Inlet in August 1861, the first naval victory of the Civil War. Stung by criticism that he did not press his victory further, and that some Confederate ships had run his blockade, he retired to Brooklyn in late 1861.

CI24A

CI24A *Bouillon Bowl and Cover*, c. 1870
Diameter: 7 inches
Loan: Anonymous

This bouillon bowl with alternate panels of flowers and figures on a rich green and gold scrollwork ground has roundels decorated with a shield and the initial "B." It was made for the Bailey family of New York and Newport.

CI24B *Photograph*, 1868
Dimensions: 16¼ inches by 14¼ inches (including frame)

CI24B

Loan: The Collection of Kingscote, property of the Preservation Society of Newport County, Newport, Rhode Island

This photograph of the partners' house in Shanghai of Russell & Co. of Boston, New York, and Shanghai was taken in 1868. It shows David King, Jr., of Kingscote, Newport, Rhode Island, on the veranda (center with hand on urn). It is interesting to compare this picture with the photograph taken some twenty years later (cat. D4).

CI25 *Plate*, c. 1879
Diameter: 8¾ inches
Loan: Dr. John Quentin Feller

This dish is decorated at the rim with a tight floral and leaf design in a bright rose palette. A brilliant flat fish in the same palette,

CI25

but with a strong measure of rich greens, typical of the 1880s, is in the center. Former President and Mrs. Ulysses S. Grant acquired such a service with platters and plates in 1879. Nellie Grant Sartoris, their only daughter, inherited the service. It eventually passed to the Peabody Museum, Salem, Massachusetts. This plate is thought to belong to that service.

Reference: John Quentin Feller, *The Canton* Famille Rose *Porcelains* (Salem: Peabody Museum, 1983), 16.

CI26 *Vase*, c. 1870
Height: 28 inches
Loan: National Park Service, Home of Franklin D. Roosevelt National Historic Site (385)

This vase, of a shape known as *yen yen*, is decorated with a tree, branches of white prunus, and birds on a black background. The decoration uses translucent enamels of the early eighteenth century in a style now known as *famille verte*. Many attempts were made to copy this ware, particularly in the early and late decades of the nineteenth century. This is a fine example of such a copy. Warren Delano, a China trade merchant who knew the country well, brought it back about 1870.

Warren Delano married Catherine, a daughter of Joseph Lyman. He died in Hyde Park in 1900. Delano's youngest daughter, Sara, born in 1854, married James Roosevelt in 1880. She was James's second wife and died in 1941. Their only child, Franklin, born in 1882, became the thirty-second president of the United States.

CI27 *Vase*, c. 1870
Height: 35½ inches
Loan: National Park Service, Home of Franklin D. Roosevelt National Historic Site (369)

Unlike the *yen yen* vase illustrated above, this cylindrical vase with a sloping neck and out-turned, overhanging, pierced petal rim is of a shape which only gained popularity about 1870. The ground is a pale green celadon glaze; the figures are in underglaze blue and white enamels. Warren Delano brought this vase with him from China.

CI26

C127

CI28

CI28 *Miniature Table Screen*, c. 1850–1880

Height: 11⅜ inches
Loan: National Park Service, Home of Franklin D. Roosevelt National Historic Site (326)

This miniature screen of five panels is made of wood covered with velvet decorated with gold thread. Matching pairs of scenes appear on the side panels; the central panel has the figure of a juggler. The screen probably had no functional purpose, but sold as a novelty for a side table in a late nineteenth-century drawing room. Warren Delano probably brought it home from China about 1870.

CI29 *Canton Enameled Box*, c. 1870

Length: 4⅛ inches
Loan: National Park Service, Home of Franklin D. Roosevelt National Historic Site (1154)

This brightly enameled box with flowers on all sides shows copper at the edge of its rectangular lid and at the base. Warren Delano brought it back from China about 1870. A label on the box records that it was in Franklin Roosevelt's bedroom when he was a boy at Hyde Park.

CI30 *Sea Chest*, c. 1850

Dimensions: 20½ inches by 14¼ inches by 13½ inches
Loan: Dr. Alan Granby
Photograph: Hyland Granby Antiques, Dennis, Massachusetts

Mother of pearl and wood inlay carved over the lid and three sides cover this sea chest. When the lid is lifted, the front panel releases and falls forward revealing four drawers, each inlaid with a diamond pattern, and four top compartments. Another "secret" compartment is hidden behind the wooden inlaid panel above the drawers.

The chest formerly belonged to the Philips family, relatives of Robert Dimon, whose shipyard, Smith and Dimon, built the *Sea Witch*. Tradition holds that Captain Robert H. Waterman of this famed clipper ship was the original owner. The chest was

CI29

C130

C131

apparently made for him in Canton. On her maiden voyage, the *Sea Witch* sailed from New York to Hong Kong in 104 days; her record return voyage took 74 days, 14 hours. The vessel was wrecked off the coast of Cuba in 1856.

C131 *Ship Model, twentieth century*
Length: 41½ inches
Height: 28⅝ inches
Loan: Dr. Alan Granby
Photograph: Hyland Granby Antiques, Dennis, Massachusetts

This twentieth-century scale model of the *Flying Cloud*, one of the most famous clipper ships of the American China trade, illustrates two of the principal features of the China clipper, the simplicity of line and the spread of sail. Donald McKay built the *Flying Cloud* in 1851 and sold her to Grinnell Minturn and Co. of New York, whose flag she flew for years. She was 225 feet in length and displaced 1,793 tons. Her main yard was 82 feet; her main mast was 88 feet. Josiah Perkins Creesy served as her first captain and completed many fast runs between New York and China. Her record of 89 days from New York to San Francisco via Cape Horn was never equaled. In 1863 Grinnell Minturn and Co. sold the *Flying Cloud* to James Baines. A fire destroyed her in St. John, New Brunswick, in 1874.

C132 *Gouache on Pith Paper, third quarter of the nineteenth century*
Dimensions: 8 inches by 12½ inches
Loan: Mr. Keith Lindsay Black, New York

This pith painting is one example from five albums of them included in the exhibition. Each of the albums originally contained twelve paintings from the same series; the five series are on flowers, fish, birds, boats, and festivals or ceremonies. Pith paper, made from the papyrus plant, is extremely fragile. Few examples survive in good condition. The pith paper was commonly bordered by silk ribbon and mounted onto the album leaves.

While these albums are unsigned, many others carry the signatures or shop labels of well-known Chinese painters. These pith painting albums were studio productions; several artists worked on each painting. The albums were sold inexpensively, and were very popular souvenir items for tourists throughout the later nineteenth century. They were also exported in large quantities for sale in America.

CI32A

CI32B

CI32C

CI32D

The Last Century of the American China Trade, 1880–1984

DI *Advertisement*, c. 1885
Dimensions: 11⅛ inches by 14 inches
Bella C. Landauer Collection, The New-York Historical Society

A. A. Vantine and Co. of 827 to 829 Broadway was among New York's principal retail outlets for goods imported from China. This poster illustrates a porcelain teapot, a bronze vase, paper lanterns, and an umbrella stand. The store's annual catalogues usually contained a number of pages of goods from India, China, and Japan. One page illustrated a "Medallion" punch bowl (today, "Rose Medallion") and lists six different patterns—including "Medallion," "Imari," and "Tokio"—and fourteen sizes. A Medallion punch bowl, 11½ inches in diameter, was priced $8.00; a bowl 16 inches in diameter cost $16.00. A 19-inch Imari bowl cost $18.00. The least expensive bowl was a "Sedji," 14 inches in diameter, which was priced at $4.00.

DI

D2 *Photograph, Shanghai*, c. 1890
Loan: China Trade Museum, Milton, Massachusetts

Nineteenth-century Americans had widely varied tastes in tea. To serve them, the

Great American Tea Company of 51 Vesey Street, New York, offered the following varieties in 1863:

Hyson	*$1.15 per pound*
Young Hyson	*$0.90 per pound*
Imperial	*$1.15 per pound*
Gunpowder	*$1.25 per pound*
Imperial Twankay	*$0.80 per pound*
Japan Tea (uncolored)	*$1.00 per pound*
Twankay	*$0.50 per pound*
Oolong	*$0.80 per pound*

Careful blending was the key to profitability. This photograph shows the tea-tasting department of Geo. Macy Tea Company of Shanghai, c. 1890.

D2

D3 *Two Paintings*, c. 1890
Dimensions: 8½ inches by 11½ inches (approx.)
Medium: Watercolor on paper
Loan: China Trade Museum, Milton, Massachusetts

After the treaty which ended the Taiping Rebellion in 1863, occidentals were increasingly able to travel to China. The wives of missionaries and merchants made journeys which would have been impossible in earlier decades. These watercolors by Isabel Forbes, the wife of Frank B. Forbes, a merchant trading with Boston and New York and the Swedish vice consul, are entitled "Upcountry China." (Shown on p. 140.)

D4 *Two Photographs, Russell & Co.,* c. 1890
Loan: China Trade Museum, Milton, Massachusetts

These photographs of Russell and Co.'s partners' house at Shanghai were taken a few years before the firm closed in the 1890s. The partners lived in comfortable style. Contemporary paintings of the houses along the river in Shanghai attest to their comfort and opulence. The roominess of this residence contrasts sharply with the cramped quarters half a century before in the factories at Canton. (Shown on p. 140.)

D5 *Three Photographs*, 1896
Loan: China Trade Museum, Milton, Massachusetts

After the bankruptcy of Russell and Co., the Tomes family lived at Gough Hill on the peaks in Hong Kong. Charles Alexander Tomes had been a partner in Russell and Co. These three photographs illustrate their friends, family, and home in 1896:

   a) *Charles Alexander Tomes (right) and two friends*
   b) *Charles A. Tomes and his wife, Hettie Hancock Tomes, with their three children and a friend*
   c) *The veranda at Gough Hill in 1896.*

(Shown on p. 140.)

D3

D3

D4

D4

D5A

D5B

D6 *Coins*, 1797–1903
Loan: American Numismatic Society,
New York

One Peso, Mexico, 1889
One Peso, Philippines, 1903
One Trade Dollar, Great Britain, 1903

(Not illustrated.)

D5C

Chinese merchants normally preferred
payment in silver rather than kind. Their
preference required western merchants to
carry considerable quantities of silver
bullion as well as the silver coins of many
nations. Since value depended on the
weight and purity of the silver, a Chinese
moneychanger examined and weighed each
coin and stamped it to certify it. The coins
in this group are all so marked. Their
dates span more than a century, although
they might well have been used together.
For minor transactions, Chinese currency
was used. The most common of these coins,
a copper piece with a hole in the center,
was called a "cash." The modern term
"cash" derives from this coin.

The coins exhibited are:

Eight Reales, Bolivia, 1797
Eight Soles, Bolivia, 1848
Two Reales, Spain, 1811
One Dollar, Hong Kong, 1868
One Trade Dollar, United States, 1878
One Yen, Japan, 1894

D7 *Plate*, c. 1900
Diameter: 9⅜ inches
Loan: Anonymous

This plate is probably not part of a service,
but made for display. The portrait is taken
from an early nineteenth-century engraving. The poorly painted polychrome border might be of any date between 1880 and
1915. The type of painting bears comparison
with the two plaques illustrated below.

Robert Fulton was not a native of New
York, although many of his later triumphs
were connected with the state. He was born
in Pennsylvania in 1765. At the age of twenty-two he visited England, meeting such
people as the Duke of Bridgewater, who
was famous for his canal. After experiments
to improve lock gates, in 1793 Fulton con-
ceived the idea of propelling ships by steam.
By 1797 he was in Europe again, this time
France, to study submarine explosives. It

was here that he at last perfected the earliest
steam ship. He returned to the United
States in 1806. In 1814 he constructed the
first U.S. war steamer. Later the same year
he improved his submarine torpedo. He
died in 1815.

Whether this plate commemorates the
centenary of his return to America and tri-
umph of 1806, or his death in 1815, or some
other date, is not clear.

D7

D8

D8

D8 *Two Porcelain Portrait Plaques*, c. 1909
Diameter: 10¼ inches
Loan: Anonymous; Grand Union Tea Co. advertisement, c. 1895, Landauer Collection, The New-York Historical Society

Painted in orange, sepia, and black, these two portrait plaques were probably made in Canton about 1909. The portraits are of William Howard Taft and James Sherman of New York, elected as President and Vice President of the United States respectively in 1909. The lettering on the Taft plaque has been overpainted or altered, but careful examination shows the name "Taft."

The occasion of these two plaques is not clear, but other examples have not been reported. The portraits are clearly taken from contemporary photographs. The tea advertisement, c. 1895, with the portraits of Cleveland and Thurman shows how easily the Chinese might have obtained such originals.

D9 *Chinese Bond*, 1911
Dimensions: 22 inches by 14½ inches
Loan: R. M. Smyth & Co., Inc.

In an effort to stimulate the national economy, early in the twentieth century the Chinese government floated many bond issues backed by American financial institutions. This 1911 bond supported the construction of railroad lines in the provinces

of Hunan and Hupei. Four New York institutions backed the issue: J. P. Morgan and Co., Kuhn Loeb and Co., First National Bank of the City of New York, and National City Bank of New York. (Not illustrated.)

DIO *Pair of Elephants with Spill Vases,* 1983
Height: 9½ inches
Loan: Mrs. Mildred Mottahedeh

These elephants, naturalistically colored with brightly enameled spill vases on their backs, are copied closely from earlier models exported from China, particularly in the period 1790 to 1810. In the Orient the original vases held incense tapers; in Europe and the United States they often held wooden spills for use in lighting pipes from the fireplace.

These reproductions have been made in China at the suggestion of Mottahedeh Inc. of New York, for many years a pioneering firm in the reproduction of Chinese porcelain. Until recently, most of the firm's reproductions have been made in Portugal. In cooperation with the Chinese government, however, Mottahedeh Inc. has been making an increasing number of pieces in China itself, where special facilities have been made available. The Chinese have welcomed American advice on suitable Oriental designs, for despite centuries of experience in the manufacture and export of porcelain, they have relied for generations on Western shapes, patterns, and initiatives.

At the outset, it was the originality of new shapes and designs from China rather than their resemblance to occidental products that encouraged Europeans and Americans to buy porcelain from the mystical East. Perhaps new initiatives such as this one can once again breathe excitement into the American China trade. (Not illustrated.)

THE NEW-YORK HISTORICAL SOCIETY · INSTITUTED 1804

This book was set in various sizes of Baskerville type by Joan Romano and Jean Wagner on a photocomposition system. Laszlo Matulay, Abraham Mittelmark, and Jean Wagner prepared the pages from a design by Quentin Fiore, who also designed the cover. The text was printed on eighty pound Mohawk Superfine paper while the cover was printed on one hundred pound Quintessence cover stock. Halliday Lithograph of West Hanover, Massachusetts, printed and bound this book. New York and the China Trade *was prepared by Columbia Publishing Company, Inc., of Frenchtown, New Jersey, which also supervised its manufacture.*